TREES IN THE LANDSCAPE

TREES IN THE LANDSCAPE

Graham Stuart Thomas
OBE, VMH, DHM, VMM

FOREWORD BY LADY EMMA TENNANT

INTRODUCTION BY DOUGLAS CHAMBERS

SAGAPRESS, INC.
Sagaponack, New York

*To my friends on the Staff of the National Trust
who have taught me so much
and who may wish they had taught me more*

FIRST PUBLISHED 1983
COPYRIGHT © GRAHAM THOMAS 1983

JONATHAN CAPE LTD, 30 BEDFORD SQUARE, LONDON WCI

REVISED EDITION PUBLISHED IN NORTH AMERICA 1997
BY SAGAPRESS, INC., SAGAPONACK, NY
PRODUCTION CO-ORDINATED BY CAROL LEWIS
PRINTED IN HONG KONG
DISTRIBUTED BY TIMBER PRESS, PORTLAND, OREGON

LIBRARY OF CONGRESS CATALOGING-IN-PUBLICATION DATA
Thomas, Graham Stuart.
    Trees in the landscape / Graham Stuart Thomas; foreword by the
Lady Emma Tennant: introduction by Douglas D.C. Chambers.
        p. cm.
    Originally published: London: Cape, 1983. With new foreword and
introd.
    Includes bibliographical references and index.
    ISBN 0-89831-035-0 (hard)
    I. Ornamental trees. 2. Landscape gardening. I. Title.
SB435.T462 1997
715'.2--dc2I   97-7951
                                                                    CIP

CONTENTS

COLOUR PLATES

Picture Credits

For permission to reproduce photographs the author and publishers are grateful to the following:

Acland, Sir Richard, Bt, p.33 above

Aerofilms, p.21

British Library, p.45

British Museum of Prints and Drawings, p.51

British Transport & Holiday Association, p.56

Brooks, Col. C.A. Atfield, p. 40

Cambridge University Collection, p.27 below

Country Life, pp.31, 119 above

Courtauld Institute of Art, pp. 28, 29

Jenkinson, Andrew M., pp.12, 13

Kersting, A. F., p.48

Muskett, J. A., p.72 above

National Museum of Wales, The, pp.50 above, 74

National Trust, The, plates 6 and 9, and pp.20, 25, 27 above, 28, 29, 33 below, 37, 38, 39, 41 below, 46 left, 48, 49, 50 below, 55, 61, 72 below, 75, 76, 109, 115, 116, 119 below, 154, 167

Ordnance Survey, p.46 right

Victoria and Albert Museum, plate I

The reproductions of plates from the works of Humphry Repton are by kind co-operation of the Lindley Library of the Royal Horticultural Society; these include the trophies of tools on pages 3 and 193. The engraving on page 141 is taken from *Forest Trees of Britain* (1894) by C. A. Johns. The drawing on page i is the author's personal logo.

The remaining photographs are by the author.

FOREWORD

I am delighted to welcome a new edition of Graham Stuart Thomas's masterly book, *Trees in the Landscape*. Mr. Thomas's international reputation is based on his work as a nursery-man, as Gardens Adviser to the National Trust, on his rescue of many once-neglected old-fashioned roses, and on his books, which cover many aspects of gardening. But though he is best known for his plantsmanship, Graham Stuart Thomas is much more than a gardener. Like William Kent in the eighteenth century, he "leapt the fence and saw all nature was a garden".

We live on one of the world's most beautiful islands. It is well-endowed with naturally interesting and sometimes dramatic scenery which over the centuries has been embellished by the hand of man. Landscape which to the untutored eye appears entirely natural is often the result of thoughtful planting carried out by our forebears, who knew how to combine use and beauty beyond the boundaries of the garden. One of Graham Thomas's aims in writing this book is to revive the quiescent art of landscape gardening.

There are many telling photographs in *Trees in the Landscape*. One shows the tree which inspired the book. A handsome ash, bare-branched in May, dominates the view of a mountain valley in North Wales. The picture shows how immensely valuable a single tree can be. Mr. Thomas reminds us that the very word 'landscape' is derived from a Dutch artists' term meaning a painted view, which gradually came to mean the countryside that was depicted rather than the picture itself. He quotes from the eighteenth and nineteenth century masters of the art of planting, particularly Humphry Repton, who coined the phrase 'landscape gardening' and defined it as 'the pleasing combination of art and nature adapted for the use of man'.

Though Mr. Thomas rightly enjoins those who currently bear the great responsibility of choosing and placing trees to do so with an artist's eye, he is also immensely practical. He has spent a long life-time growing plants, and he knows that it is futile to plant a lime-hater in an alkaline soil, or a moisture-lover on top of a chalk down. His annotated list of trees and shrubs suitable for landscape planting and for temporary screening is full of wise advice. "The copper beech is an upsetting sight in our green landscape..." and he says of Lawson's Cypress, "Its formal outline precludes its use in the landscape except as a temporary screen." He warns planters to keep exotic species in the garden, where they belong, and says that though "it may please some to decorate the landscape with such lesser trees (as Sorbus), so doing will negate all that Repton and Jekyll have taught us."

In our own century, as Mr. Thomas points out, mature trees and woods have been admired but neglected. The situation has improved recently. The National Trust has carried out dramatic restorations of historic landscapes at such places as Fountains Abbey, Stowe, and Wimpole, as well as planting vast numbers of trees in its parks and on its agricultural estate. The traditional improving land-lord still exists, and is now helped by the government's Countryside Stewardship scheme. Local authorities and their landscape architects are currently responsible for the appearance of much of the country, especially in the environs of schools, hospitals, industrial estates and new towns. The government, through the grants it administers, has recently begun to encourage farmers, who often know little about forestry, to plant more broad-leaved trees on their land. And the Forest Authority and Forest Enterprise, successors to the Forestry Commission, are at last trying to follow best practice as pioneered by Dame Sylvia Crowe's work for the Commission before the war. The re-issue of *Trees in the Landscape* is timely. Everyone who is responsible for planting trees should be grateful to Graham Stuart Thomas for making available the distilled experience of a lifetime.

Lady Emma Tennant
Chairman of the Gardens Panel
of the National Trust

A Note from the Author

Though this book was originally written with British landscapes in mind I have been at pains to pay due regard to the immense wealth of trees derived from the Eastern States of North America. A whole chapter is devoted to them. No other area of the Temperate World has provided so rich an inheritance of trees noted for their fall colour. Not only is this in quantity but also in col-oration, embracing fiery hues as against the prevailing yellows of the Northern European forests. Fortunately these American species from comparably similar latitudes are equally at home in Britain as in related climates in the United States.

This is the first book that has been written on this subject for almost 200 years.

G. S. T.

Introduction to the 1997 Edition

Trees in the Landscape is about how tree-planting makes landscapes happen. By framing the countryside, trees are both the lens and the subject of the landscapes they enhance. Like painting, from which the word 'landscape' takes its origin, there are many colours and textures in the arboreal palette. Graham Stuart Thomas ranges through them with the love of an artist, but an artist who has 'painted' himself with this medium and knows it at his fingers' ends. In his hands what might be a simply practical manual is deepened by a love of countryside, an intimate knowledge of trees, and an awareness of the difficulty of getting the business of planting just right.

Writing about one of his predecessors, William Robinson the great exponent of wild gardens, Thomas praised him for having enriched the landscape with trees and tree planting. Robinson was not original in doing this, but he was instrumental in the late 19th-century movement to see gardens as part of landscapes, a movement in which trees were an essential element in the recovery of a rapport between culture and nature.

America discovered this rapport in the middle of the 19th century. Once the wilderness no longer seemed simply threatening, the ancient trees that had been the settlers' enemy became the hallmarks of the homestead. Even the surviving primeval forests were eulogised as the shrines of American antiquity in the writings of Emerson, Thoreau and Muir. The dark and savage forest of Hawthorne gave way to the noble sublimity of Fennimore Cooper's wilderness. And the sublime forests of the Hudson River school of painters prepared American sensibilities for the lofty grandeur of Yosemite's forests. It was this cultural shift that made possible the arboreal visions of Downing, Vaux, Eliot, Todd and Olmstead: forested wildness in the midst of cities.

It took an aesthetic revolution to produce the climate that led to the creation of these parks But an earlier English revolution had preceded it, a revolution in attitudes to landscape and to trees in particular. From their English forbears Americans inherited these new tastes and began to put them into practice as early as the 18th century at such estates as Mount Vernon and Monticello.

This revolution can be traced to several sources: Milton's celebration of an arboreal Eden, tufted in lofty trees, in his *Paradise Lost*; the arcadian landscape paintings of Claude Lorrain with their idyllic groves; and John Evelyn's extremely influential book, *Sylva*, which mixed practical advice with spiritual justifications for planting trees. The section of Evelyn's book called 'An Historical Account of the Sacredness of Standing Groves' revolutionized English attitudes to trees in the landscape throughout the eighteenth century.

It would have been impossible to create the landscape garden without the palette of majestic trees. A landscape garden cannot be created with marigolds. 'Praise a large garden, but cultivate a small one,' the Roman poet Virgil wrote, but English owners and designers of the 18th century were more inclined to the former and enclosed their newly acquired acreage with vast tree-lined rides.

The eye had also to be taken out to the perimeters of these new estates in carefully arranged stages: through the clumps first suggested by William Kent but used to perfection by Capability Brown. Brown was attacked by his contemporaries for destroying avenues of trees, but he only softened their rigid lines and made them seem more naturally part of the landscape. One of his patrons even feared that Brown would denounce him as an infidel for having removed some of the trees on his own estate.

With this landscape revolution came an interest in the shape, colour and texture of trees. As a result, so many American trees were imported into England that by the end of the 18th century there was a craze for 'American Gardens'. Between 1700 and 1750, 61 new trees came into England, most of them from America's eastern seaboard. Cottonwoods *(Populus trichocarpa)*, tulip trees *(Liriodendron)*, white pines *(Pinus strobus)* and black walnuts *(Juglans nigra)*, all were sought after by gardeners who believed that the first stage of an estate ought to consist of tree-planting. As a consequence certain areas of southern England came to look like idealised American landscapes.

Graham Stuart Thomas writes about the importance of graduated colour in tree planting, and this too was an 18th-century concern. John Bartram's patron, Peter

Collinson, called landscaping with trees 'painting with Living pencils.' And Philip Southcote preceded Capability Brown in seeing that the landscape should be composed like a painting: a meadow in the foreground, a winding stream in the middle ground, and clumps of trees to lead the eye to the background. Moreover he spoke of using different gradations of colour in planting deciduous trees than in planting evergreens.

Graham Stuart Thomas is especially fond of the work of Brown's successor, Humphry Repton. Repton's sensitivity to what his contemporaries called 'the genius of the place' was a distinguishing feature of his use of trees in the late 18th and early 19th centuries. In Jane Austen's *Mansfield Park* it is a sign of the stupid vulgarity of Mr. Rushworth that he thinks that Repton would recommend destroying the fine old avenue of trees on his estate at Sotherton. As Thomas points out, one of the longest avenues of trees in England (through Clumber Park) was planted on Repton's recommendation. But then Mr. Rushworth does not even understand one of the basic dictums of the 18th-century landscape: look up to woods and down to water.

For those of us who not only read about landscapes but make them, Thomas's is a voice of wise counsels. In a landscape shaped by trees, he observes, 'fifty years is a long time in anticipation, but short in retrospect.' Gardening on this scale is usually a matter of slow metamorphoses, though a devastating epidemic like Dutch elm disease or a new motorway can suddenly wipe the canvas and ask for new solutions. Here Thomas's 'Practical Points in Regard to Planting' can be read by any landscape gardener with the wit to translate his general recommendations about height and shape and speed of growth into the vocabulary of locally available trees. Our threatened elms are more handsome than any in Europe and it is our pines and firs that first astonished European eyes. We have our own hawthorns and maples and beeches in North America, and where cypress will not grow, the elegant shape of the columnar cedar *(Thuja occidentalis 'Mahonyana')* will serve.

Thomas's estimable common sense also comes from practice. He knows that tree guards are necessary, but he also knows how to conceal them. And he knows the enormous value of shelterbelt plantings to break the force of the wind; as much an enemy to gardens in the coastal areas of England as it is in much of North America. Nor is he naive about the problems of restoring old forests or reinstituting a nature that is no longer appropriate to landscape that man has been altering for thousands of years. What he has to say of Britain is also true of America: there is no returning to 'unspoiled wilderness'.

Beautiful woodlands are works of art, not nature. If they are to be successful, they must be as carefully arranged as a rose garden-another area of expertise for which Mr. Thomas is famous. Probably the most beautiful created landscape in the part of southern Canada where I live is a thousand acres of re-planted forest that evokes what the painters of that landscape have taught us to see as beautiful and sublime. In such a landscape, what is most important is not primarily the individual trees but the unity of overall effect.

This too is an old subject. Sir William Chambers, one of the 18th-century creators of the Botanic Gardens at Kew, objected to specimen plantings when their overall effect in the landscape was distracting. His bugbears were the holm-oak (*Ilex*) and weeping willow (*Salix babylonica*). Thomas's is the purple beech (*Fagus sylvatica var. purpurea*): a handsome enough tree on its own near the house but a sore thumb in any larger landscape. Although he thinks kindly of the odd exotic specimen as an incident, he is as aware as Sir William of the dangers of this sort of planting, and his overall recommendations are for congruency.

'First follow nature' was another 18th-century recommendation, and it is the one with which Thomas concludes. When he writes about trees as the means by which the garden is joined to its larger landscape he places the labours of all of us inside the context that makes them meaningful.

Douglas Chambers

APPRECIATION

Many great gardens look out upon parkland, farms or natural scenery. This is very true of some of the noted gardens of the National Trust and in many instances consideration of the view has influenced our planting in the gardens, and indeed *vice versa*. With our garden properties I have been familiar for over a quarter century, but gardens form only a very small proportion of the thousands of acres of countryside owned by the Trust. I felt it desirable for this book to have direct reference to some of its great tracts of country but have had no opportunities to visit and study them all.

When I mentioned my predicament to our Chief Agent at the time, John Gaze, he was on the point of retiring; he had been working for the Trust since 1948, in the southern counties, in Devon and in the East Midlands before becoming Chief Agent. He very kindly agreed to provide an annotated list of some of the larger and more interesting properties, which will be found on pages 170-82.

For this he has my very sincere thanks, but this act of his is only an example of how he has been helping us all for so many years. My thanks are also due to my many colleagues who have ransacked their archives and stores of photographs. These augment so well my own photographs which depict native trees and scenery obtained *en route* from one garden to another and during short holidays.

My thanks are also due to the Librarian and his staff of the Lindley Library of the Royal Horticultural Society, who have as always been wholeheartedly helpful.

Lastly I take pleasure in thanking once again Margaret Neal who has so accurately interpreted the scribble of my MS.

G.S.T.

This book is for the country house, or any place where there is woodland, or land to plant; its object is to get people, after thought of the needs of a true garden, to think more of their woods from aesthetic and other points of view. The hard and ugly lines so often seen ... and which often come from modern ways of fencing ... have no reason to be. The artistic eye soon finds them out ... The only true test of all such things is the artistic one – Do they make for ugliness or beauty?

William Robinson
from the introduction to *The Garden Beautiful,*
Home Woods and Home Landscape (1907)

1   *"The Valley of the Stour" by Constable. See facing page.*
2   *Clun Castle, Shropshire, a beautiful grouping of trees but how much improved it would be if the trees on the slope immediately in front of the castle were cleared.*

3   This beautiful meadow scene near Church Stretton, Shropshire, is enlivened by the well-placed Lombardy Poplars.

4   The lake at Blickling Hall, Norfolk. A placid scene but lacking in perspective owing to the absence of foreground planting.

5 The Field Maple (Acer campestre) is a useful small tree, prettily tinted in spring and autumn.

6 The early autumn picture at Stourhead, Wiltshire, which stresses the extreme contrast obtained from planting silvery willows (Salix alba) against the dark green of conifers.

7 *A photograph taken in May in North Wales. It was this splendid ash tree, not yet in leaf, in its perfect setting that inspired me to make a collection of British tree photographs; this book is the direct outcome.*

8 *The danger of planting Douglas and Silver Firs among native broad-leafed trees is shown forcibly; as soon as the firs spear up into the wind they develop ugly tops. The light green is the spring foliage of a Red Oak (*Quercus rubra*).*

INTRODUCTION

Woodland countries are interesting on many accounts. Not so
much on account of their masses of green leaves, as on account of
the variety of sights and sounds and incidents that they afford.
Even in winter the coppices are beautiful to the eye, while they
comfort the mind with the idea of shelter and warmth.

William Cobbett (1762–1835)

Stephen Switzer, in his *The Nobleman, Gentleman and Gardener's Recreation*
of 1715, records that King Charles II said how "He liked those Gardens or
that Country best, which might be enjoy'd the most Hours of the Day, and
the most Days in the Year, which he was sure was to be done in ENGLAND,
more than in any country whatsoever." To enjoy either countryside or
gardens we need comfortable greensward to walk upon, or paths, so that
we can take in the beauties of the immediate or distant surroundings. These
could be mountains or hills, running or static water, ancient or new buildings, the flowers and shrubs of our borders, or a garden seat. Not one of
these can be fully enjoyed without trees. Trees, except in the tiniest of
gardens, are the prime ingredient of a beautiful view.

Switzer was writing, as did others later, in the expansive eighteenth
century, for landowners of varying quality, in whose demesnes were trees
perhaps in great quantity. Some of us today have plots scarcely big enough
for anything larger than a fruit tree. We garden with our eyes mostly on the
ground or only a few feet above it. And yet we in Britain are all the time
conscious of great trees around us, peopling the landscape in our mind's eye.
It is difficult for us to imagine the countryside without trees, though in some
parts of the world regrettably the opposite is true.

There is no doubt that trees are necessary to us, for both body and soul.
In the intensively farmed areas of the south and east of England trees are
becoming more scarce. As old trees die in the hedgerows they are not
replaced; indeed the hedges themselves may be ripped up. Forestry and
agriculture are equally at the mercy of successive governments and as a
consequence the planting of trees in spinneys and woods is of fluctuating
profitability, and thinning and husbandry become neglected. In fact in the
south-eastern part of the country there are undoubtedly far more trees per
acre in built-up areas than there are on farming estates. Thus in an odd
sequence of events we increase the number of trees in general as fast as we
increase urbanisation.

A side-effect of this is the extraordinary way in which creatures of the wild – foxes, hedgehogs and birds – have come to live and forage in those same built-up areas. Here they find food and shelter which is lessening in the farmed areas. Therefore we should encourage our trees and wild bushes wherever we can in the countryside, providing greenery, spinneys, clumps and similar features so that wildlife can as far as possible roam freely and need not venture into domesticated areas where it can live only an artificial existence.

Of late years we have been exhorted to plant trees. It is a tremendous responsibility to plant any but small garden trees, and even the planting of these requires a great deal of forethought. In planting a large-growing tree we are as likely as not jeopardising something else. If in fifty or a hundred years it has become too large it may have to be felled or lopped, or it may push over a wall, render a building unsafe, block or rupture drains, interfere with overhead wires, impede traffic, or merely obstruct the light. Councils today, in many parts of Britain, are very keen to preserve what trees are

Carding Mill Valley, The Long Mynd, Shropshire, from a lithograph of c. 1840, entitled "The Factory, Church Stretton". See facing page.

growing, even, apparently, at the expense of the safety of a new building, and certainly without considering the potential growth of a tree. Neither is the suitability of a tree always taken into account. It is a waste of time and money to put a preservation order on a poor, ill specimen of a tree which is no asset to either the property or the neighbourhood. In an area scheduled for development, a tree may be "preserved" only to be killed later by having its roots cut to make way for a drain, or by having the level of the land adjusted. Some architects object strongly to having trees left or planted near to buildings, others approve of either or both. This planting or preserving of trees is, as I have said, a tremendous responsibility; in order to arrive at a proper decision in either instance we need to know the tree concerned and to be able to assess its potential growth on the particular soil and siting, both *above and below ground*. During the last ten years there have been many ridiculous examples of tree planting for the sake of planting a tree: a Copper Beech, for instance, planted so that it will totally obscure – and even envelop – a beautiful church tower; a Tulip Tree placed 0·7 m

Carding Mill Valley, 1981 (National Trust). The factory is still present, also the manager's house in front of it. A view typical of many parts of our countryside, where "development" over the years has resulted in incongruous buildings, power poles and lines. The Lombardy Poplars pierce and tend to dwarf the noble skyline. The power poles need screening. Self-sown sycamores abound and in fact the present abundance of trees obscures the view without screening anything apart from the pole on the right bank.

(2 ft) behind the wall of a school and only 7·5 m (25 ft) from the building; a weeping willow in a small front garden, or several planted in a municipal thicket only a few feet apart – but the list could be interminably lengthened.

So far, apart from *Gardens of the National Trust* which touched upon the landscape and countryside, my books have been written almost entirely for gardeners. For many years I have itched to write about trees; my memories of journeys about the country are punctuated by great trees seen from the road, in hedgerow, park or garden. They are like old friends; I know that one such will appear round the next bend of the road and it is a real sadness when I see a loss has occurred. For years I had almost worshipped a great Black Italian Poplar near Bridgnorth, Shropshire, but one day it had fallen. Perhaps even more hurtful to the senses is the discovery of the damage caused by inexpert lopping on a splendid giant of a tree, whose only fault was that its branches were perhaps too near the top of the tractor hood.

In maturity at least, all nature's trees are beautiful, though some garden forms and hybrids are not. Unfortunately human greed today invades our choice and we forget that green is the most important of all colours; our choice in gardens is often swayed by the brilliance or size of flowers, or the un-greenness of the foliage. It is greedy to want a splendid tree to be decked all over in brightly coloured flowers, and a sign of boredom with natural beauty to want a tree to have foliage other than green. Too great a brilliance, or too much of it, will create a sense of surfeit in years to come. The trees, like the lawn, are the framework and background to our colourful shrubs and border plants.

But this is not a book about gardening – though it has a chapter devoted to this pursuit – nor is it a book simply about trees. There are plenty of books about both and I should hesitate to add to the latter category, on which subject some superlative books have been written during the last ten years or so. Neither is it about forestry, nor farming – it is about trees used in a sensitive or artistic way to create or re-create beautiful landscapes. And, so far as I am aware, this is a subject that has had little attention for about 180 years – since Humphry Repton wrote his books.

In my work for the National Trust my advice has frequently been sought for the planting or replanting of an area outside the garden proper. It may have been simply a question of providing a belt of trees to ward off the prevailing wind and shelter the house and garden. More often than not it was a consultation on the replanting of the park or landscape and especially on the prospect from the house. After many years' work I was invited to give a talk to my colleagues on the subject, and this book is the outcome of the notes used at the time, considerably elaborated. The National Trust's staff is a wonderfully annealing body of men and women who quickly shoot down those who presume too far, and perhaps it is just as well that at the time of my lecture I had not delved into Repton's books and so was not

A view of the Conwy River at Tal-y-cafn, North Wales, at low tide when the mud banks diversify what would otherwise be an overwhelming expanse of water. The woodlands on the left flow down the slopes attractively. To the right of the middle of the photograph, some felling would not only break the horizontal line of the trees but would reveal more valley beyond. For a really balanced picture a large tree or clump is needed in the right foreground.

able to quote the following observations from *Sketches and Hints on Landscape Gardening* (1794): the "faculty of *foreknowing effects* constitutes the *master* in every branch of the fine arts; and can only be the result of a correct eye, a ready conception, and a fertility of invention, to which the professor adds practical expertise"; furthermore, "the painter, the kitchen gardener, the engineer, the land agent, and the architect, will frequently propose expedients different from those which the landscape gardener may think proper to adopt."

Repton was under no illusions as to his expertise in landscape gardening and we are fortunate to have his several books which set forth in so unequivocal a manner all his maxims and disciplines. In reading them I am

FARM *and* PARK

Two pictures from Repton's Observations, *1805, to demonstrate the difference between farm and park. Note the absence of horizontal lines in the lower picture.*

struck by the fact that in the world of landscape planting he is exactly the counterpart of Gertrude Jekyll in gardening. There are the truths and the stumbling blocks set out clearly for us all, and the artistry of the one is equalled by the other's.

It was Repton who coined the expression "landscape gardening". He wrote, again in the *Sketches*:

> To improve the scenery of a country, and to display its native beauties with advantage, is an ART which originated in England, and has therefore been called *English Gardening*; yet as this expression is not sufficiently appropriate, especially since Gardening, in its more confined sense of *Horticulture*, has been likewise brought to the greatest perfection in this country, I have adopted the term *Landscape Gardening* as most proper, because the art can only be advanced and perfected by the united powers of the *landscape painter* and the *practical gardener*.

This shows how he differentiated between pure horticulture – the growing of fruits, flowers and vegetables in an area set apart for them – and the wider concept of the governed landscape. A hundred years or so later Miss Jekyll taught us how to apply the Reptonian principles of colour and form in the landscape to pure horticulture. She was in the main dealing with smaller areas. Neither Repton nor Jekyll was in any way ashamed of being termed a gardener, and neither would have invented the term "landscape architect".

It may be apposite at this point to ask a practical question. Where are the landscapes that need rethinking? Are there enough landowners to make it worth while to write a book like this? As I intimated earlier, in the properties of the National Trust there are many great prospects across parkland to be considered. Further, they have almost without exception suffered from neglect over the last hundred years. Likewise there are many great estates still in private hands in a similar state of need. There are many great houses no longer owned by the family who shaped the landscape with trees – now perhaps converted into apartments, or adapted to the needs of institutions; usually when the parkland has passed into other hands, some of it remains in the form of "grounds" and these need wise handling if the semblance of surrounding parkland is to be fostered. It is high time that our schools and colleges also gave thought to this matter. They should plan ahead, so that there are always young trees coming on and that surrounding screens do not disintegrate. But it is not only the great estates and houses that need new ideas; there are large stretches of coastline, hills and downs, farmland and park separate from great houses. These need looking at with an eye for the future, and not only in terms of farming and forestry. It is encouraging to read that the Country Landowners' Association has established the fact – by sending out a questionnaire – that a vast quantity of trees has been planted

Approaching Glendalough, County Wicklow, Eire. The suave lines of the hills are spoilt by three things: the hard lines of shed and walls in the foreground, the crossing lines of the walls dividing the water-meadows into unnecessarily small compartments, and the clutter of small trees in the meadows.

since 1945, that these are being managed with conservation in mind and that those landowners so inclined are also engaged in preserving and indeed encouraging hedgerow trees. This is all good evidence that the country as a whole is not unaware of its needs.

There are much newer concerns, large factory sites, municipal playing fields and open spaces, most of them in built-up areas which cry out for some softening of the surroundings; airports, new towns, man-made deserts and the like come to mind. Mown grass and Floribunda roses are not the only answer to tar and bareness – the eye needs a rest as well as excitement on leaving a day's work inside a building, and a rest is best given by natural scenery or something like it. It is this so-called natural scenery, man-made but comforting to the eye, which should be encouraged.

In these pages I am accordingly trying to lead the way to a revival of a quiescent art. We have absorbed the Jekyllian maxims in our gardening; it is, I think, time to go back further and absorb the Reptonian maxims for the benefit of our landscapes and countryside. After all, there are those who claim it is Britain's major contribution to art in general. We still have a lot of it left from the eighteenth century; should we not revitalise our landscape art? Apart from the long-term beauty to be achieved I am certain that young people respond to growing beauty and would quickly grasp the need for careful thought in planting.

This book is intended to show how "to improve the scenery of a country, and to display its native beauties with advantage". To devote oneself to these aims calls first for a general review of the countryside and then an evaluation of the trees at our disposal. We in Britain have a limited number of native species, and my aim is to show how this number, supplemented by a very few exotics, can be used to capture every possible variation of height, light and shade necessary to create a picture. It would be much easier to do this if we allowed ourselves the latitude of choosing from the vast numbers of species of trees – many of which have settled down as natives – to augment our palette. If we were planning to plant a garden instead of seeking to re-create the countryside, that is what I should recommend. Where would our gardens be without exotic shrubs and plants? But while we have become accustomed to an almost indigestible richness of fare in our gardens – as in our home furnishing – our landscapes could not be re-created legitimately by the use of exotics to gild the highlights and increase

A lake in North Wales. On the left of the picture the drumlin slopes are somewhat obscured by spotty trees; if these were kept to the hollows the hillocks would be accentuated. In the centre, the winding road gives life to the picture. Rather than keep the fence and scattered trees on the dividing line between the two central meadows, the two could be thrown into one. On the right of the picture, by trimming up the big ash tree, more meadow could be seen.

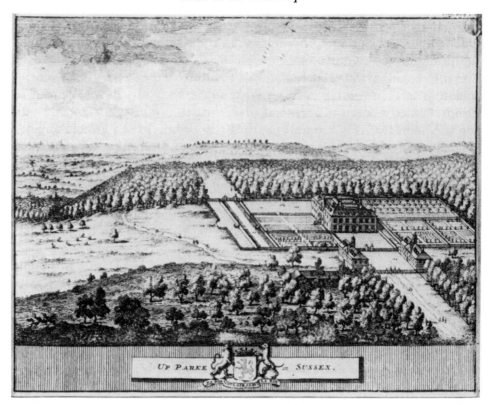

The house at Uppark, West Sussex (National Trust), was built c. 1685; the approach was between two pavilions reaching the house on the east side, as depicted by Johannes Kip, above, about 1720. The pavilions were demolished about 1750 and replaced by the existing pair, as shown in the aerial photograph on the right. In 1810 Humphry Repton brought in a new approach-drive between these later pavilions on the north side. His terraces on the south side are just discernible, projecting far from the house. To frame these, and to help protect the garden and house, the Trust has planted belts of Holm Oak to the south-east and the south-west of the house. The two curved hedges have been removed since the photograph was taken.

the shadows. We should merely create something quite different, and it is my belief that in our soft-lighted climate the softness of our native trees is best, with a touch here and there of some other tree from among a few which, by long usage, we have become accustomed to relate as much to the countryside as to our gardens.

The gardening profession came into being rather late in the day and so I intend calling on writers and artists for their thoughts and reactions through the following pages and in Chapter 10. These thoughts mostly accrue, it should be noted, not from studying a wild landscape, natural forest, call it what you will, but from contemplating the contrived landscapes of the eighteenth century, which were created with an eye to beauty but often limited by more practical considerations. Landscape gardeners may be taken to exercise their talents with an overall view deriving from a painter's eye but tempered by practicalities. Comparing the painter with the landscape gardener in his *Fragments*, Repton wrote, "The former sees things as *they are*, the latter as *they will be*. Indeed I have frequently observed that, in planting a tree, few persons consider the future growth or shape of different kinds. Thus the beech and the ash will admit of a view under their branches, or will admit of lower branches being cut; while the fir tribe and conic shaped trees will not." Let us, therefore, return to the eighteenth-century appreciation of beauty coupled with use – perhaps best combined in gardening, landscape planting and architecture, and to a lesser degree in other arts – and see what can be done with the materials available to create or re-create our landscapes.

1

A SHORT HISTORY OF THE LANDSCAPE

We have manie woods, forests, and parks, which cherish trees abundantlie, although in the woodland countries there is almost no hedge that hath not some store of the greatest sort, besides infinite numbers of hedgerows, groves, and springs, that are maintained of purpose for the building and provision of such owners as doe possess the same.

R. Holinshed (c. 1520–80)

Mankind has been on earth for such a short time that it is surprising, even appalling, that these pages - concerned with the restoration of the beauties of the landscape - should need to be written. Geologically, the Ice Ages occurred quite recently, and our trees, shrubs and plants spread northwards as the ice receded from the rest of Europe, until our separation from the mainland by the waters of the Channel some 10,000 years ago. The beech arrived before this happened; it just "scraped in", as it were, before the watery gates closed, in time to become one of our most superb trees and one which with the oak gives our landscapes their special quality. The Scots Pine was dying out in England when the beech came in, though farther north, in Scotland, it has remained an established native. Early settlers moving in from the Continent brought other trees with them, such as the chestnuts and the Sycamore, whose heavy seeds could not be spread by wind but only by animals or man. All these are now looked upon almost as natives.

Although certain trees such as the magnolias, the European Larch, the Norwegian Spruce and many others were here before the Ice Age, they never returned afterwards to re-colonise the country once the climate had again become suitable for them, because of the Alpine barrier and the Channel. However, our present climate, tempered by the warm waters of the Gulf Stream and shaded by prevalent clouds, gives us the right conditions for growing trees from all over the Temperate Zones, both North and South. For these reasons our gardens, parks and arboreta flourish, to say nothing of our lawns; fortunately, we are rarely subject to extreme temperatures and our lands have not yet been made barren by the activities of goat or man.

We can therefore envisage this country slowly recovering its tree-clad appearance after the recession of the ice; but ever since the first human settlers arrived, they have been increasingly engaged in the felling and removal of trees over most of the country. Only occasionally have there been spurts of planting, as in the late seventeenth century, the eighteenth century and since the afforestation programme began in 1919. It is difficult to think how mankind could have existed – particularly in our chilly climate – without trees; trees for warmth, to make tool handles, rudimentary dwellings and furniture, fences, gates and bridges. Ever since the first nomads penetrated the natural countryside, brushwood and trees have been felled for one use or another. If we accept that our land had over most of its area a thin to dense growth of trees, we can perhaps begin to imagine what "virgin forest" means; true "forest", in the sense of wild land, unploughed and unplanted, and certainly not afforested, is scarcely visible in any part of Britain today. It has been posited that the New Forest in Hampshire comprises some of the least touched natural growth of trees in these islands, perhaps in Europe; Hatfield Forest and the Forest of Dean approach it in this ancient perspective. This was the kind of land most popular with the Norman kings, who started the vogue for vast royal forests for hunting

Contrast of tree shapes: solid Horse Chestnuts, delicate ash and pollarded willows at Grantchester, Cambridgeshire.

their imported fallow deer, and also with the scattered populace who needed it for their cattle and pigs.

There is strong evidence, however, that even in those early days a system akin to woodmanship, as Dr Oliver Rackham so aptly calls it, was practised. It was a big job to fell a great tree with the axe or early saw, but by "coppicing" (that is, cutting down young trees and allowing them to sprout until ready for cutting again – over perhaps a five- to fifteen-year period), small wood for burning, fencing and early building was readily obtained. Where the young shoots might suffer from browsing, the coppicing was done higher up, above the reach of animals, when it is termed "pollarding" – a method which has found favour with painters of landscapes, who have contrasted the stumpy outline of pollarded trees with flowing streams. "Shredding" is the term used for the annual trimming of the stems of tall trees to provide fodder and wicker-work material; it is admirably portrayed in Hobbema's famous picture of "The Avenue, Middelharnis", of 1689.

By the fifteenth century agriculture had greatly developed and, later, in 1543 a Statute was passed which limited the destruction of trees and required that twelve trees should always remain per acre. This was necessary because of the increase in wood used for fuel by the ironmasters, and in the building of greater houses and ships. It was, however, popular to fell trees. Woods and forests, like mountains and rocky scenery, were not attractive to people who had much to do to provide for themselves and fend off robbers and wild animals.

The Beginnings of Our Modern Countryside

The Saxons, devoted agriculturists, had started fencing areas either by coppice-wood or hedges, or walls in neighbourhoods where stones lay loose on the ground and impeded the early ploughs. Some of their first enclosures were called "parks". (We may note that the Persians and Greeks also had their parks.) Subsequently very large areas were cleared and farmed in a limited way by a rotation of three crops in long strips; everyone joined in to lend a hand as crops matured or work became urgent. Many examples of this strip- or ridge-and-furrow cultivation remain in view today, though perhaps grassed over or partially disguised by subsequent ploughing.

The countryside as we know it began to develop its pattern of small hedged fields over tree-free areas in the seventeenth century, but later about a fifth of England was subjected to the Enclosures Acts of the eighteenth and nineteenth centuries, particularly from 1801. This resulted in roughly squared fields and straighter hedges and roads, whereas early enclosed fields followed contours and took heed of natural excrescences. Hedges and walls were built to keep livestock out as much as to keep them in: the farmer had to see that the crops were protected as well as ensuring that animals did not stray. Wire was not generally used. Whereas the tenant was entitled to the small wood from hedges and coppices, the landlord took the timber from the hedgerows and woods. Sturdy-branched hedgerow oaks provided the ideal framework for ships, and the ever-increasing demands of the navy and merchant navy caused alarm from time to time. Trees were felled all over the country and cartage was difficult to the ports. The Rev. William Gilpin (1724–1804) records that "Two or three years was not an uncommon space of time for a tree to spend performing its journey to Chatham." But towards the end of the nineteenth century iron was replacing timber for ships, and, equally fortunately, instead of employing charcoal for smelting, the art of making coke had been discovered and saved further depredations of our wooded landscapes.

Since then a vast amount of afforestation has been undertaken, particularly in the north of England, and in Scotland and Wales.

A plan of the Basildon Estate, Berkshire, a National Trust property, dated 1838, by Joshua Townsend. It shows the modest park complete with its distant woodlands, within the area of the entire estate. This is what Repton would have recommended.

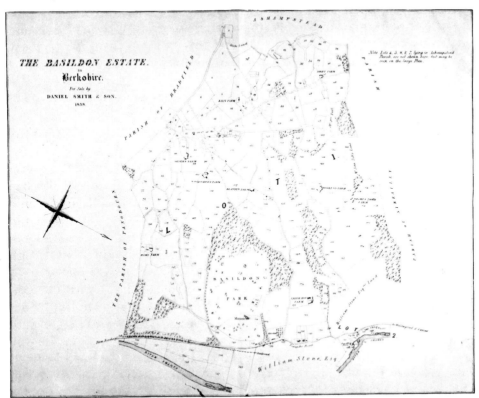

Apart from pure forestry and the nursing of coppices and pollards, our landscape – the fields and hedgerows, rough pasture, forest and woods – is man-made to a greater or lesser degree. The history of the development of our landscape has its roots in the history of the human race; in the effect of people upon land in a utilitarian sense and to a lesser extent from an aesthetic viewpoint. It is noteworthy too that as we felled our trees those "avenues of stone", our cathedrals, were being built.

During the seventeenth century and into the eighteenth century the wild forest was still considered unsafe for riding through; moreover no large native trees were planted in gardens – they were too much allied to the frightening forest. Fruit trees, on the other hand, were very popular. Garden fashions developed along strictly formal lines, fundamentally because people wanted to feel the influence of the formal house extending its safety all around, helped by walls, hedges and avenues. If the first avenues were formed by marking a way through the forest for riding, by means of stakes or the felling of certain trees, later the trees were deliberately planted to extend the garden's formal design. There was comparative safety in radial rides within sight of the house. These ideas emanated from France, where the strict lines of Italian gardens had been enlarged until in the late six-teenth century the "garden" extended into the countryside and became a park. The trees were often clipped or shaped to present a flat hedge-like result.

A start had been made at reinstating trees by planting avenues and also by preserving and increasing coppices and pollards, to say nothing of hedgerow trees, which were not only allowed to grow here and there but were also deliberately planted. (This applied particularly to the hedges of English Elm which, with their great specimen trees, until recently dominated so much of the fertile farmland.) In carving up the landscape with radial avenues, too, the intervening areas were probably thickened with trees for contrast, judging by old engravings.

Switzer, thinking of the formal designs of the previous century, wrote:

When we consider the Elevation of a well-contriv'd Seat it requires, that everything appears tall, stately, and bold; and all of it contrary to that narrow and mean-spiritedness with which Designs generally abound. It also directs, that the adjacent Country be laid open to view, and that the Eye should not be bounded with high Walls, Woods misplac'd, and several Obstructions, that one sees in too many Places, by which the Eye is as it were imprisoned, and the Feet fetter'd in the midst of the extensive Charms of Nature, and the voluminous Tracts of a pleasant Country.

Furthermore, in his *New Principles of Gardening* of 1728, Batty Langley began to lead the way from excess of formality, though he still advocated the avenue. It was not until well into the eighteenth century that any notable

9 On swampy, limy ground great variety in tints and heights can be obtained from willows and poplars.

10 The lake at Petworth, West Sussex, with an old Horse Chestnut in the foreground. A February photograph showing the value of the red–twigged willow, Salix alba 'Britzensis', when the sun shines on it.

11   *Long shadows accentuate the sloping meadow at Sezincote, Gloucestershire. The English Elms have now gone but the lake and other trees remain.*

12   *The browsing line under the Horse Chestnuts emphasises the sloping ground, but the Copper Beech strikes a discordant note.*

13   Brilliant reflection from a well-lit stretch of water in Cumbria, with Sycamores green and variegated.

14   The park at Trelissick, Cornwall. The Copper Beech is best kept within reach of the house, and not in natural scenery.

15 *View from the Lily Lake at Stourhead, Wiltshire, in spring. The slope on the right is emphasised by the browsing line and shadows; the dark green of the conifer wood recedes into the background.*

16 *A lake at Farnborough Hall, Oxfordshire, dark and mysterious with no light on it.*

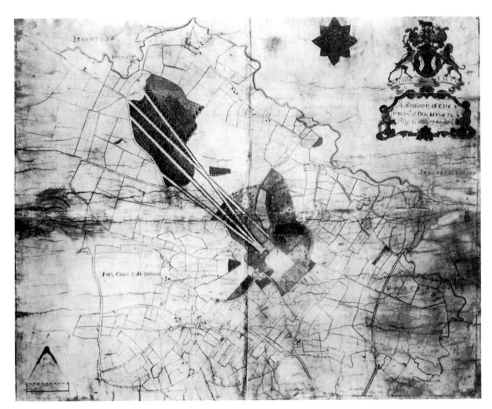

Above, avenues at Blickling Hall, Aylsham, Norfolk, a National Trust property, focused on the north-west front of the house, drawn by James Coxbridge, 1729. This type of planting survived from the fashion of the previous century and shows the influence of French avenues which led the eye to the extremes of the property, regardless of the topography. Below, part of the great avenue, 150 m (500 ft) wide, at Wimpole Hall, Cambridgeshire, a National Trust property; it was composed of elms which have died since the photograph was taken and have been replaced with Small-leafed Limes. The original avenue was planted in 1720.

change could have been detected. Influences had been at work, however, and formality lost its appeal. Repton wrote, "One great mischief of an avenue is, that it divides a park, and cuts it into separate parts."

Far from wishing to dominate the landscape with straight lines, people had at last learnt that the more or less natural landscape was a thing to be admired and enjoyed.

The Inspiration of the Landscape

With a return to more peaceful times in the eighteenth century, travel abroad became the relaxation of the wealthy fashionable set, the nobility and gentry, many of whom took an interest in matters of taste and the arts. Inspired by paintings of the previous century in Italy and France of idyllic

"Sacrifice at the Temple of Apollo", by Claude Lorrain (1600–82). This is representative of the early pictures which gave the inspiration to the English landscape garden in the eighteenth century. Note the great foreground tree which increases the perspective by its height and shadow, and the large-leafed plants in the foreground.

landscapes around classical ruins, they returned to their country seats with a desire to create similar views, to be enjoyed from their own windows. No less than the actual sight of natural beauty, of mountains, precipices, crags and torrents, the realisation that this sublimity could be captured on canvas had its effect. The term "Picturesque" was coined, a word which today is commonplace. We must give the main credit for "leaping the fence" and seeing that "all nature was a garden" to William Kent. Horace Walpole, in his essay *On Modern Gardening* published in 1780, puts the whole new scheme and appreciation of the landscape so well that I cannot do better than quote it. His words embody all that Repton later sought to teach:

> He [Kent] felt the delicious contrast of hill and valley changing imper-
> ceptibly into each other, tasted the beauty of the gentle swell, or concave
> scoop, and remarked how loose groves crowned an easy eminence

A painting by William Ashford in 1785 of the view of Castle Ward, Northern Ireland, a National Trust property. The height of the gentle hills is enhanced by their being bare, above the height of the trees in the valleys.

with happy ornament, and while they called in the distant view between their graceful stems, removed and extended the perspective by delusive comparison.

Thus the pencil of his imagination bestowed all the arts of landscape on the scenes he handled. The great principles on which he worked were perspective, and light and shade ... The gentle stream was taught to serpentise seemingly at its pleasure, and where discontinued by different levels, its course appeared to be concealed by thickets properly interspersed, and glittered again at a distance where it might be supposed naturally to arrive ... Thus dealing in none but the colours of nature, and catching its most favourable features, men saw a new creation opening before their eyes. The living landscape was chastened or polished, not transformed. Freedom was given to the forms of trees; they extended their branches unrestricted, and where any eminent oak or master beech had escaped maiming and survived the forest, bush and bramble was

A view from the Clwydian Hills towards Snowdonia. The softly rounded terrain in the foreground and middle distance is made less dramatic by the fact that, while the shapely fields are open, the valley is thickly filled with trees. Some felling is indicated. The great ash tree dominates the scene; its late leafing habit makes contrast with the other trees and bushes, already fully fledged in late spring.

At Chirk Castle (National Trust), Clwyd, North Wales, there are fine examples of a formal terrace walk and a ha-ha. It was the latter feature, derived from traditional fortifications, that enabled eighteenth-century landscapes to be viewed without the interruption of wall, fence or hedge.

removed, and all its honours were restored to distinguish and shade the plain.

There is much more in the same vein.

The new ideas of embracing the landscape and using it as a setting for the house were made possible by the adoption of the sunken wall or fence, called the "ha-ha", as a boundary. It is generally considered that the first use of the ha-ha for this purpose was by Charles Bridgeman; William Kent first caught the glimmer and attraction of natural beauty and put it to good account; "Capability" Brown extended the views, sheets of water and clumps of trees to a suave and repetitious formula; later Humphry Repton brought a more Picturesque view of things and sought to wed the garden more closely to the landscape. He was followed by William Sawrey Gilpin and others.

In the nineteenth century the trend continued in regard to the landscape: though the properties were more numerous many were of less extent. The vast stretches of countryside in the largest estates were echoed by smaller properties each with their own drive, perhaps a sheet of water, and belts and clumps of trees for the enjoyment of shooting. This all applies to the wealthy; likewise gardening in the stricter sense was concentrated in walled gardens where the craft was practised to ever greater perfection, even excess.

The great parks and indeed much of the landscape of Britain reflect the taste and changing fashions of the powerful landowners, swayed by their desires for field sports, farming and forestry. In the eighteenth century, at a time when the Enclosures made possible large schemes for land management, money was forthcoming from profits from Colonial enterprises and, later, the Industrial Revolution.

The main difference in the nineteenth and twentieth centuries in what we may now call the garden landscape, as opposed to wild forest and natural countryside, was the introduction of tall-growing conifers from North America and the Far East. The whereabouts of a great Victorian mansion can often be determined from afar today by the spires of wellingtonias and other conical tree-tops piercing the skyline of native trees. The avenue became fashionable again and was simply a form of the eclecticism which has been prevalent throughout the history of garden design.

Collections of the new foreign trees merited the term "arboretum". There are examples of the desire to wed the arboretum to the landscape at Killerton, Devon. From the great arboretum there are two fine views down and across the land, which is farmed. That to the south has been much improved by the construction of a ha-ha, so that the trees of the arboretum now seem to link up with those in the meadows without a break in the

Wellingtonias – still only comparatively young – pierce the skyline of a native oak wood. The junction of flat meadow and rising ground will always present a hard, straight division.

Three views of Killerton, Devon (National Trust), facing west from the Cross. Above, an
illustration of present and proposed plantings; the garden is protected by a ha-ha.
Below, a painting believed to be by William Tomkins, A.R.A., 1730–92.

greensward. A large new clump has been planted, and also some cedars fairly near to the house. The view to the west is towards Dartmoor; here the farming is arable and gradually during this century the whole area has become denuded of trees. As a result, not only is the outlook open and bald, but the arboretum is completely exposed to the wind. In recent years some planting has been done to improve the view.

There has been a decline in woodland management during this century, also of coppicing and pollarding, but wholesale fellings during the Great War resulted in the formation of the Forestry Commission in 1919, which organisation has covered untold acres with new trees. Thus the eighteenth-century estate planting by Brown and Repton, who aimed to create beautiful (as well as lucrative) prospects, has been exceeded in the *quantity* of trees planted in the present century; but in general the outlines of the spinney and woodland planting tend to ignore the contours and lie of the land and to be confined in straight lines. There are, of course, some notable exceptions.

The Twentieth Century

In this century we may say that woodlands have been admired but neglected, and also despoiled. Modern farming and forestry methods dominate the landscape; the fields are adapted to machinery and the hedgerow trees no longer strike so arbitrary a note in the distant prospect. Indeed the land is often divided into suitable acreages by means of wire fences. While I may repeat that there is practically no natural landscape left, except in very small parcels, the land is adapted to man's needs and fancies, and this in itself is one of the necessities of life in these islands. The ideal should be a combination of farming, forestry, ecology and landscape design, not the haphazard felling of trees, clearing of hedgerows and dotting of the landscape with trees in the odd corners which are inconvenient for husbandry. Repton inveighed strongly against this. He considered it a

> common defect of all places where hedges have recently been removed, and too many single trees are left; the natural reluctance ... to cut down large trees, at the same time that he sees the unpleasant effect of artificial rows, is very apt to suggest the idea of breaking those rows by planting many young trees; and thus the whole composition becomes frittered into small parts, which are neither compatible with the ideas of the sublime or beautiful. The masses of light and shade, whether in a natural landscape or a picture, must be broad and unbroken, or the eye will be distracted by the flutter of the scene.

There is no doubt that the eighteenth-century planters – and indeed some of later times – have added much to the beauty of the country. It is a great

Corfe Castle (National Trust), Dorset, in early spring. Above, the view is spoilt by the horizontal lines of fence and woodland on the right. The second picture indicates how this might be improved.

inheritance, and yet practically all of it is man-made. This is a fact a little difficult for the uninitiated to grasp. The fundamental difference between a completely natural open-forest type of landscape and what today we call the countryside is that the former is more or less self-perpetuating whereas the latter needs constant attention. It is not easy after long neglect to start

35

Uninterrupted farmland near Chanctonbury Ring, West Sussex. Such a bald area might be improved by clumps of trees and by accentuating the farm roads, as indicated in the second photograph.

A beauty spot in West Yorkshire near Hardcastle Crags (National Trust). This is a site that needs thinning rather than planting to reveal the course of the stream and small lake.

afresh. But in deciding to restore a beautiful prospect we have to arrest decay and plan for the future. We have to mend the frayed landscape and re-sculpt the design.

We are fortunate in having two sets of records for reference. There are the Kip engravings made at the junction of the seventeenth and eighteenth centuries which often give good guidance about the early formal landscapes, and the Ordnance Surveys of two hundred years later. These frequently show traces of the earlier design, but also record remarkably faithfully what remained of eighteenth-century landscapes and planting, old boundaries, earth-works and the like. Since then two world wars and their attendant upset of values have caused neglect.

Aesthetics First

In forming decisions for restoration, it is best to begin from an aesthetic standpoint and to consider the ideal first. The approach to the house and views from it should as far as possible be treated aesthetically, while the further reaches of the parkland can be considered more from a utilitarian point of view. But the essence of the matter is a wedding of beauty to use, adapting the landscape design to farming and forestry; we cannot as a country afford always to put beauty first and in any event art (since we are not trying to reinstate wild forest) should in all cases be related to use.

The Brownian landscape in the park at Petworth, West Sussex (a National Trust property). Note the Picturesque shapes of the Austrian Pines on the left, and the variation from single trees to clumps of large size in the prospect.

A view of Penrose and Loe Pool, drawn by Thomas Allan, from Cornwall Illustrated, *1831. Compare with present-day photograph on page 55.*

We still have many records of plantings by Brown and Repton. If we could clear-fell every tree and start afresh, it would be possible to reinstate their plans completely, visualising that in fifty years or so some result would be apparent. It is seldom possible to patch old schemes, but Brown and Repton were not inevitably right in all they did and each scheme must be judged on its own merits.

There is yet another set of records to be consulted where they exist. Apart from early engravings and snapshots from family albums, some great landscapes have been recorded by famous artists; I need only instance the pictures at Petworth House, West Sussex, a property of the Trust, by J. M. W. Turner, and John Constable's views of Dedham Vale, Essex. Turner's paintings graphically depict the beauties of Capability Brown's skilful planting in the park, which of course remains an entity though threatened with a bypass through its centre. (Such dire happenings destroyed the entity of

On the right, "The Valley of the Stour", Dedham, near Colchester, painted c. 1805 by John Constable. Above, the same view today.

the National Trust's Osterley Park some years ago by the construction of the M4 motorway.) Dedham Vale, on the other hand, comprises properties in many different hands, and thus is vulnerable to spoliation from every angle and for varied purposes. It is an area threaded through by the River Stour, with fertile farmland much enriched – at least in Constable's time – by more or less natural small woodlands and numerous trees. Like those of Turner, Constable's pictures reveal the enormous importance of light and shade – not only in the contrast of the countryside's dramatic features, but also in the moment of superlative light captured in his mind. Being so vulnerable to change both by nature and by humans, his Suffolk landscapes have altered, almost always for the worse. This has been brought home to me by Colonel C. Attfield Brooks who is campaigning for national recognition of the dangers of losing for ever Constable's views, not only through "development" but also by the well-intentioned but thoughtless planting of trees.

The vale is, when all is said and done, scheduled as an Area of Natural Beauty. Some views have already disappeared through tree growth, while others have been spoiled. So many points brought out in this book are

Dovedale, Derbyshire. Dramatic terrain which inspired the eighteenth-century artist to give full rein to his artist's licence.

Dovedale, Derbyshire (National Trust). The same view photographed during the early part of this century. Much of the contrast between trees and rocks has since become obscured by overgrowth.

reinforced by a comparison between the photograph on page 40 and the painting opposite it; the idyllic landscape has been scarred by the numerous straight lines of a rectangular sheet of water and an avenue, to say nothing of the new road. The scene of the celebrated painting of "The Hay Wain", depicting the end of Willy Lott's cottage, has lost its great trees, though young ones are growing up under the care of the National Trust. The views of this area can never be quite the same again owing to the construction of flood-protection banks which became necessary in 1953.

During the eighteenth century large areas of the forest, trees and wild country had become approved and adopted; they were also adapted to man's needs for timber and agriculture. Grazing, after the Enclosures, was united with arable farming, and the whole joined to the fair prospect from the house. Trees were no longer frowned upon, but preserved not only as youngsters but also as mature and even decrepit specimens, old pollards and the like, which added to the picturesqueness of the views. There is no doubt that the new approach to the landscape came about partly as a result of improved farming methods, with the movement away from strip-cultivation to the Enclosures. From all this began the re-creation of the landscape, where hitherto there had been nothing but destruction. It was a new art, peculiar to Britain: aesthetics closely allied to farming and grazing. As usual, Repton has apt remarks to make: "A park has a character distinct from a forest ... Park scenery compared with forest scenery, is like an historical picture compared with a landscape; nature must alike prevail in both, but that which relates to man should have a higher place in the scale of arts."

17 and 18   Left, Rowan or Mountain Ash (Sorbus aucuparia) in Wales, bright with berries in August. Right, Wild Cherry or Gean (Prunus avium), a quick-growing tree of medium height, brilliant in flower and autumn colour.

19   A wild Crab Apple (Malus sylvestris) in mid Wales. It is an attractive small tree, beautiful in flower and in fruit, suitable (like the Rowan) for the fringes of plantations.

20 and 21   Left, the Grey Poplar (Populus canescens) bearing catkins in spring. It increases by suckers. Right, the Grey Poplar in summer. Note its yellowish bark.

22   A meadow specimen of English Oak, essentially a tree of rounded outline.

23   *A Sycamore at Saltram Park, Devon, which has achieved an exceptional size and majesty.*

24　Populus × canadensis 'Serotina', the Black Italian Poplar, is of very uniform growth, but when grown in clumps this defect is not so noticeable.

25　The foreground poplars are Populus × canadensis 'Robusta' already in reddish leaf in April. The far line of trees is of Populus × canadensis 'Serotina' as yet only in catkin. Few other trees would obscure the pylons so quickly.

2
THE HANDLING OF THE LANDSCAPE

Here waving groves a chequer'd scene display,
And part admit, and part exclude the day; ...
There, interspers'd in lawns and opening glades,
Thin trees arise that shun each others shades.
Here in full light the russet plains extend:
There, wrapt in clouds, the bluish hills ascend.

Alexander Pope (1688-1744)

In his *Fragments on the Theory and Practice of Landscape Gardening* of 1816, Humphry Repton gives us some thoughts that are particularly relevant today:

The Art of Landscape Gardening is the only art which every one professes to understand, and even to practise, without having studied its Rudiments. No man supposes he can paint a Landscape, or play an instrument, without some knowledge of Painting and Music; but every one thinks himself competent to lay out grounds ... or to criticize on what others propose without having bestowed a thought on the first principles of Landscape Gardening or Architecture.

   That these two Sister Arts are, and must be inseparable, is obvious from the following considerations. The most beautiful scenes in Nature may surprise at first sight, or delight for a time, but they cannot be interesting, unless made habitable; therefore the whole Art of Landscape Gardening may properly be defined: The pleasing combination of Art and Nature adapted for the use of Man.

His understanding of the Art came not so very long after the controlled formal efforts of the seventeenth century; in his *Sketches and Hints on Landscape Gardening* of 1794 he was already laying down guidelines to help us in our endeavours:

The perfection of *Landscape Gardening* consists in the four following requisites: First, it must display the natural beauties, and hide the natural

43

The scattering of trees in the middle distance disturbs the tranquillity of this meadow and valley view, so pleasingly divided by walls flowing down the contours. The hillside indicates how regeneration colonises the varying depths of soil. On the way to Lake Crafnant, North Wales.

defects of every situation. Secondly, it should give the appearance of extent and freedom, by carefully disguising or hiding the boundary. Thirdly, it must studiously conceal every interference of art, however expensive, by which the scenery is improved; making the whole appear the production of nature only; and, fourthly, all objects of mere convenience or comfort, if incapable of being made ornamental, or of becoming proper parts of the general scenery, must be removed or concealed.

Burke, in his *Inquiry into the Origin of our Ideas on the Sublime and Beautiful*, Part 18, claims that "No work of art can be great, but as it deceives; to be otherwise is the prerogative of Nature only." As if in corroboration, in his *Sketches and Hints* Repton suggests that "We plant a hill, to make it appear higher than it is; we open the banks of a brook, to give it the appearance of a river; or stop its current, to produce an expanse of surface; we sink the fence betwixt one lawn and another, to give imaginary extent."

The materials at hand are trees, shrubs, grass and water; together they are three-dimensional, with breadth, length, and height. To these dimensions we must add *time*, time for growth and consummation of ideas. The whole thing has as its basis the study of mass and void.

Archives

Before any schemes are approved it is advisable to study deeply the history of the property and its landscapes, the local traditions, the climate and the soil; to these should be added the future use of the farmland and woods, and the provision of shelter for livestock (if any) and for the house and garden. Nothing should be done in a hurry; it is a good plan to watch the site for a year at least, to gauge all the difficulties and possibilities and to see how the various warring interests overlap. Landscapes for different houses will remain as distinct as the houses and gardens themselves if all aims are considered carefully, and together. It is only when artistry or utility is ignored that two landscapes ever begin to look alike, but as a rule the lie of the land makes a fundamental difference anyway. Brown's landscapes have sometimes been dubbed repetitious and this is mainly because he held so closely to art alone in every property.

Hatchlands, Surrey. A plan of the park prepared by B. Armitage in 1767. The entrance is on the west side of the house. See also illustrations on page 46.

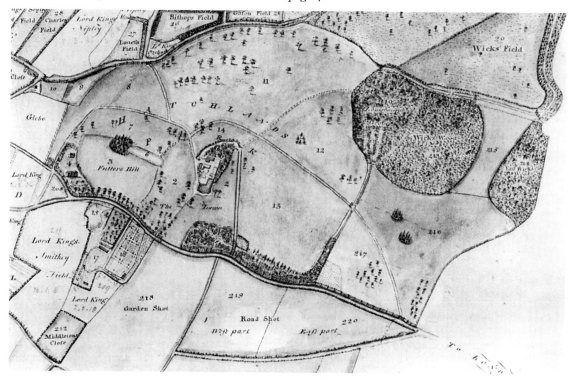

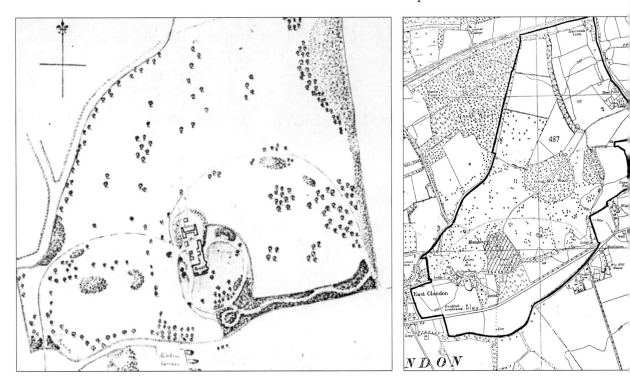

Hatchlands, Surrey. Left, Repton's plan for new drives and planting in the park, c. 1800. Right, a plan of the park in the early twentieth century, after the alterations to house and park by Mr H. S. Goodhart-Rendel. It shows the main entrance through Great Wix Wood from his pair of lodges to the entrance to the house on the eastern side. The plans of Hatchlands, a National Trust property, above and on the preceding page show how landscapes can be altered during different ownerships.

The ideally placed house in its park should have an easy approach, with diverse scenic attractions *en route*. The prospect from the house should, in large properties, appear to be limitless, with no boundaries in view. In lesser properties much the same ideals obtain and the use of shelter belts and screens can soften or obscure the boundaries. But the ideal has always been to make the boundaries *appear* to be limitless and the same aim is found in gardens to a lesser degree. Even the suburban fence can be made less obtrusive with climbing plants or shrubs. Extensiveness is not all, however. In the seventeenth century, limitless radial views were the fashion. Sometimes today one radial view may still survive, but in looking at a landscape from a given point we can best absorb an oval expanse, with the narrow end to the eye: to allow one long oblique view to unbalance such a comfortably rounded panorama is to court disaster, and, equally, one long central view, if narrow, is foreign to the scheme.

Dramatic Terrain

Because we are attempting our treatment of the landscape through the play of mass against void, it is necessary to think boldly. In dramatic terrain, with great contrast between the levels and the heights, the heights are best left bare. Where the terrain is gently undulating the heights can be accentuated by clumps of trees or a whole wooded skyline, so long as the planting spills down the slopes to call attention to them. Here are Repton's thoughts on the matter, from his *Observations on the Theory and Practice of Landscape Gardening* (1803):

> In recommending that the hills should be planted, I do not mean that the summits only should be covered by a patch or clump; the woods of the

Two pictures from Repton's Observations, *1805, showing how rather dull parkland planting can be made Picturesque by thinning woodlands.*

Most visitors to Trelissick, Cornwall, a National Trust property, know the beauty of the park-like slopes from the house to the estuary. In this reverse view of the gently undulating terrain, greater importance has been given to the low hills by crowning them with trees. Photographed in 1954, since when the Silver Firs, breaking the skyline with their scraggy tops, have been felled. In contrast the rounded tops of the Monterey Pines blend with the native trees (see detail, below).

A closer view of Trelissick, from the Historical and Topographical Survey of the County of Cornwall *by C. S. Gilbert, 1820, before the house was altered. Compare with illustrations on facing page.*

valleys should, on the contrary, seem to climb the hills by such connecting lines, as may neither appear meagre nor artificial, but following the natural shapes of the ground, produce an apparent continuity of wood falling down the hills in various directions.

In contemplating an undulating or hilly landscape the eye first takes in the heights, and next the flat, whether of grass or water. Water, whether moving or still, holds the eye longest. The slopes therefore are the places for tree planting, the more so where they are steep and thus unsuitable for any form of farming. According to the height of the highest ground, the tree planting can finish when there is, in effect, at least a tree's height of bare hill to be seen above the planting; conversely the tree planting can ascend and go over the hill if it be low, thereby accentuating the height. Either scheme can be designed to offer the greatest contrast to the meadows or lake, whether these be in the foreground or on a disappearing level. Examples of gentle heights being accentuated by a capping of trees may be seen at Stourhead, Wiltshire; Killerton, Devon, and Trelissick, Cornwall.

49

Nestling below the hill, the house at Killerton, Devon (National Trust), is seen here as sketched by Peter Richard Hoare, c. 1820. The clump of trees adds considerably to the height of the gentle hill.

A closer view of Killerton from the same angle today. The conifers of the nineteenth century are piercing the canopy of native trees and William Robinson's terrace wall, built early in this century, completely severs the arboretum planting from the park from this viewpoint.

Stourhead, Wiltshire, a property of the National Trust. A water colour by F. Nicholson, c. 1813, of a view of the lake from Six Wells Bottom, showing also how trees give added height to a low hill.

Flat Land

The flatter the land the less of it should be taken into view. In Repton's words, "Where the ground naturally presents very little inequality of surface, a great appearance of extent is rather disgusting than pleasing, and little advantage is gained by attempts to let in distant objects." Grassy meadows, either flat or undulating, were often termed "lawns" in the eighteenth century.

On land which is almost totally flat the only height is given by trees and in a way the planting becomes simpler. The greater the size of the near trees, the bigger the contrast they will make with the meadow and also with trees in the middle distance. Trees far away will seem quite small. On terrain such as this the tree heights *and their shadows* are of vital importance but they must not overshadow the dwelling or the water.

Three pictures from Repton's Observations, *1805. The top shows the browsing line uniform over flat land. The second is of the flat meadow planted with groups of trees. The third shows these same tree groups mostly fenced and underplanted; this obscures the uniform browsing line and helps to unite the small spinneys with the woodland background.*

On hilly land a browsing line is very effective. Small deer and sheep will keep the line very low; large deer, cattle and horses will give a much higher result. It is noticeable to what a regular level animals prune the low shoots. A browsing line calls attention to the slopes, and offers a dark platform to the woodland or tree clump. It is yet another attractive factor in seeking to alleviate monotonous flat pasture, though on such terrain it can have its dangers because the eye can roam to the extremity of the view. Thus the trees do not screen distant low buildings and fences. If necessary, these can of course be screened by shrubby growth, but parkland is seldom absolutely flat and if some trees are planted *in the hollows* the browsing line will be correspondingly lower and so a screen will be created. An opportunity for doing this occurred at Shugborough, Staffordshire, when it was necessary to obscure parked cars from the approach drive. By leaving some trees free to be browsed and others fenced in clumps, a variety of growth can be achieved.

Water

The valleys or lowest ground in particular are best left open, with perhaps a few scattered trees mostly in the foreground to give contrast of height. At Hatchlands, Surrey, trees are dotted through the valley with a consequent minimising of the contrast of the flatness with the very gentle undulations. At Farnborough Hall, Warwickshire, a misguided planting of Black Italian Poplars in the early 1900s has dwarfed the valley, lessening the reflective value of the water and posing trouble for the future when the trees will fall and break the banks of the historic formal ponds. Flat pasture is a beautiful contrast to slopes; in some places of course the horizontal element will be stronger than the vertical because it is supplied by a sheet of water. Repton maintained that "the beauty of a lake consists not so much in its size, as in those deep bays and bold promontories which prevent the eye from ranging over its whole surface." This is particularly noticeable at Stourhead, Wiltshire.

It is a comparatively simple matter today, with modern machinery, to dredge a lake or to create a new one. The greatest value of water in the landscape is as a reflector of light. For this reason, except in steeply sloping landscapes, it is important to have not only the foreground free, or almost free, of trees, but also the background. The value of certain lakes is minimised by the gloomy reflection of a wood. The disposal of spoil in the creation of a lake can easily be accomplished by the construction of a dam, which should in all cases follow the lie of the land; any artificial lines should be obscured by a clump of trees. Spoil from dredging an established lake is more difficult to dispose of, but it can often be used to advantage to accentuate gentle rises, or in hilly areas it can be placed at the foot of slopes and graded upwards. At Claremont, Surrey, where there was no land available to take the spoil from dredging, the extent of the lake was shrunk by a yard or so and the mud piled behind campshedding. It has now merged well with the original shore line. On the other hand there was space available at Westbury Court, Gloucestershire, where the spoil was piled about 60 cm

The contrasting effect of morning and evening light on the same view. From Repton's Observations, *1805.*

Penrose and Loe Pool, Cornwall. The scenery has altered very little since Thomas Allan's drawing of 1831 (page 39), although the hard hedge-line and the thickened trees now obliterate the slope of the land to the water. Also the fields' straight boundaries on the right could well be softened. A property of the National Trust.

A view of Rydal Water, Cumbria (National Trust). The eye, having at once taken in the tranquil lake, finds the heights bare, with trees thinning out as the hills rise. A winter or early spring picture in which the groups of pines are distinct and dark.

(2 ft) high over a very wide area. It took at least a year to dry out and revealed large cracks in dry weather; it has now settled down, however, and supports a good lawn and knot garden.

A flat meadow can be enhanced by tall trees, which will cast long shadows at morning and evening. It is usually more satisfying when the placing of some great tree or trees breaks the otherwise expansive view, but a lot depends on the size of the tree-growth and its placing. As in a garden, we should not be able to see everything at once, and a clump of trees which impinges on the flat expanse can often defeat the eye's attempt to follow the sward or water to its eventual conclusion; thus is born the desire to move and see more of what we feel is there. The lake at The Vyne, Hampshire, is shrouded by trees in this way.

The whole question of water needs separate appraisal from the practical point of view; there is no point in arranging new planting in scale with the water if silting is in progress. This has to be tackled not only to restore the sheet of water that ought to be there, but to prevent a recurrence of the silting by diversion or collection. I recall one extraordinary occurrence at Winkworth Arboretum, Surrey, where there is a spillway between two lakes; the water had torn away so much soil from its short course – rather out of sight – that within a space of ten years or so it had built up an island where it entered the lower lake.

Fences and Boundaries

The marring of a landscape by fences is an old sore. Repton inveighed against it. He maintained that, where fences were vitally necessary, they

From Repton's Fragments *of 1816. "The* BELT *when it has outgrown its original intention, can only be broken effectually by large and bold openings; because by leaving a few trees the line of Belt still remains; especially when marked by a hedge or permanent fence." Of the lower picture, Repton wrote, "This sketch also shews the effect of letting light on the Water, by removing the dark reflection of trees."*

Distant larchwoods flow down the hillside pleasantly near Stanway, Gloucestershire, while tall foreground trees produce shadows which emphasise the gently undulating valley floor. The fence increases the perspective and brings a human scale to the scene.

26 *The Black Poplar (Populus nigra betulifolia) in Monmouthshire. A male form, with crimson catkins in spring. Note its heavy, arching branches. Often known as the Manchester Poplar.*

27 *The Small-leafed Lime (Tilia cordata) in flower in Shugborough Park, Staffordshire. This is looked upon as one of the best substitutes for the English Elm.*

28 *A group of White Willows in Herefordshire, the silvery undersurfaces of the leaves upturned by the breeze and catching the sunlight.*

29 *Pollarded White Willows in flower in early April.*

30   A natural stand of Scots Pines near Loch Torridon, Scotland.

31   The Common Ash (Fraxinus excelsior) *has pale, putty-coloured bark, conspicuous against other trees. A storm was brewing at the time of this photograph.*

*32 Red-twigged willows (Salix alba 'Britzensis') with an underplanting of red Dogwood
(Cornus alba) photographed near Stockbridge, Hampshire, in February, lit by the sun.*

*33 The Crack Willow (Salix fragilis) is a bushy low tree whose twigs even in winter are dense
enough to make something of a screen. Photographed at Dorchester-on-Thames, Oxfordshire.*

should flow down the slopes and never follow the contours. There is no doubt that this is a wise principle. Nothing so destroys the lie of the land as straight hedges or, worse still, fences which cut the slopes in two. On the contrary, an artificial line whether of hedge, fence or wall, or the edge of a wood or spinney, which flows down a slope calls attention to the slope and, where the contours are gentle, has the advantage of accentuating them.

There are at times apparently insoluble difficulties between the landscape artist and the farmer on this issue. As a rule a farmer, whatever he grows, will divide his land with fences at points where one level, or one type of soil or microclimate, gives way to another. It is natural to his outlook that these lines of hedges should in many places *follow* the contours; it is here that age-old ditches occur in many areas, carrying surplus water from the slopes away from the flat land. These difficulties are, however, not insuperable; with a little give and take they can be overcome to the lasting benefit of the prospect.

With regard to fences themselves there is no doubt that the old iron park-rails are ideal. Split wood lasts longer than sawn wood and this is one of the reasons for using the traditional post-and-rail fencing. This is, however, quite unsuitable near to a formal classical building, and is best kept for the outer countryside or in relation to farm buildings; it was particularly obtrusive at Clandon Park, Surrey. Now that sawn timbers can be tanalised, their life has been immeasurably lengthened and the more sober, sawn post-and-rail fencing can be used for many positions.

Tricks and Devices

There are various tricks that can legitimately be employed in parkland planting, where it will be remembered aesthetics should be *considered* first, and where the desire is to create the effect of a limitless landscape, whether it be small or large. It is a well-known trick in eighteenth-century and later engravings to show in the foreground a clump of Burdock, dock or other large-leafed plant; nothing increases the sense of perspective so much, even on flat paper. As a general rule great houses stand on an eminence, looking down on to meadows or a lake and then away and up to the rising ground. This indicates that the land in the foreground may be marshy and this in its turn suggests that the soil is moist enough for *Gunnera* (for large landscapes), Burdock, the Great Water Dock or *Heracleum*. Likewise by planting large-leafed trees near to the eye a similar result is obtained. Sweet Chestnut, Horse Chestnut or plane are all large-leafed; if trees such as oak, beech, Hornbeam and ash are chosen for the middle distance, finishing with Field Maple, pine and fir, the gradation of leaf-size will accentuate the perspective and make a small landscape appear quite large. *Heracleum* grows near the water at Blickling Hall, Norfolk, and a London Plane has been planted nearby; the lake is a mile long so that large trees look quite small already in the distance.

Other tricks to feed the eye are to decrease the size of the trees from, say, the plane to the thorn, but this is seldom possible or permissible, and the same applies to avenues whose lines converge in the distance. If carried to excess it becomes a joke, but if the avenue is only observed from one end a slight narrowing would be effective in providing an idea of greater length.

This deception can be practised with animals just as with plants. I well remember my first visit to Knightshayes Court in Devon. It was a spring evening and the light was beginning to fail. From the terrace there is a magnificent prospect down sloping meadows and fields and I noted the majesty of the great trees. On looking out of my window the following morning the trees seemed bigger than ever as they towered over the black animals in the distance, apparently cows. I discovered later that Sir John Amory at that time kept black *sheep* and it was these which had caused such exaggerated perspective in my eyes!

It is important to employ objects in the landscape to enhance the feeling of its being in use and man-made. This is why walls, fences and gates assume so great an importance and must be appropriate to their surroundings. A distant building can make or destroy the perspective just as much by its colour as by its size. A small white cottage or barn will reduce the perspective; a stone-coloured cottage or barn, whether small or large, will have the opposite effect. (Examples can be seen at West Wycombe Park, Buckinghamshire.) This is an important point because the whole art of the landscape gardener is to increase the perspective, thus making the landscape appear larger rather than smaller.

Colour and Texture of Foliage

The use of different coloured greenery to increase the perspective is not so much a trick as a skill. Among light greens for the foreground are the planes, Tulip Tree, White Mulberry and *Acer negundo*. (I always feel grateful to the chance or forethought which placed dark Turkey Oaks and limes behind the remarkable Oriental Plane at Blickling.) Among deciduous trees those of lighter tone merge gradually into the mid-greens of Hornbeam, the oaks, limes, ash, and Horse and Sweet Chestnut. In the far distance the soft, dense, dark greens of yews, pines and firs seem to melt away in their dusky contrast, which can be linked to the general use of deciduous trees such as Turkey Oaks, whose foliage is of a very dark green. Trees of much lighter tone, to be used sparingly perhaps to pick out the whereabouts of a particular feature such as an island or promontory, or to give light relief to a belt of dark greenery in the distance, are the White and Grey Poplars, White Willow and Whitebeam. They are all soft in effect and scarcely obtrusive, and they

A near-perfect view in the Peak District of Derbyshire, from Edale End Farm, a National Trust property. The intrusion of wall, fence (though in need of repair when the photograph was taken) and farm buildings gives a human touch to the extensive landscape.

are not comparable to trees with variegated foliage, nor those with coppery purple tones, which cannot be used in the landscape without giving an exotic result. These are best kept to the garden and in the immediate vicinity of certain houses, but one needs to keep a firm rein on one's fancies in this respect. The only large tree with variegated leaves that, at a distance, will lose its markings and give a uniform light green tone is the Variegated Sycamore, as at Stourhead, Wiltshire, and Arlington Court, Devon.

Glossy leaves likewise need some care in placing. Seen near at hand the Common Cherry Laurel reflects a great deal of light: in the middle distance it presents a chopped, muddled effect. The holly, with its smaller and twisted leaves, has much the same result but in a lesser degree. The Holm Oak or Ilex is a tree of great value, but is disconcerting because for ten months of the year it is a very dark green; when in late May the young foliage opens it is a sulphury silver. This is specially noticeable where many grow together, as in the Ilex Grove at Cliveden, Buckinghamshire.

As a general guide to the use of colours and tints of green, greater contrast is permissible in the south-east of the country, where the light is stronger. In the cooler west and north the softer grey and dark green tones of the willows and pines strike a more sympathetic note.

Shapes of Trees

Humphry Repton recommended using round-headed trees as a contrast to Gothick buildings and pointed trees with those of classical design. We must remember, however, that his pointed trees would comprise Lombardy Poplar, European pines and firs, and that the great influx from the Far East and West of conical conifers had not yet reached our shores. His precept is open to discussion if one thinks of the effect of trees other than in contrast; a building of late Gothick pinnacles and chimneys may be said to be enhanced by or at least in harmony with conifers, whereas the (by now) very English prospect of a Georgian house may be deemed cosily and suitably embowered in native, round-topped trees. Repton was in any case more susceptible to the charms of exotics than Capability Brown, who used almost exclusively the natives, with a preponderance of beech and oak.

The skyline of a clump or belt of trees is important. Planting for an eventual imitation of the gentle outlines of Brown, one is compelled to use those trees which will form a united canopy and wind-pruned outline, such as beech, oak, Turkey Oak, Sweet Chestnut, Small-leafed Lime, Sycamore, Norwegian Maple and Hornbeam. Great woodlands of such trees echo in their skyline the gentle chalk hills and many other undulations of the British landscape. Trees which do not form this close-cropped line are the Broad-leafed and Common Limes, ash, *Nothofagus* and most conifers, the exceptions being Scots and Austrian Pines, and Eastern Hemlock. This latter category of trees is best used in small groups and clumps. It is unsatisfactory to use tall-growing conifers where their greater height will spire through the native canopy. The Douglas Fir and the Silver Fir are notable offenders, producing ugly, wind-swept, wispy tops well above oaks and other trees among which they have been planted; the effect is of course exaggerated on rising ground. They were long an eyesore at Trelissick, Cornwall, and Mount Stewart, Co. Down. Nobody knows to what height the Wellingtonia will grow in Britain. Many already over 40 m (140 ft) are still growing strongly. Their height makes a mockery of our native vegetation and for this reason they are best planted in valleys – where, incidentally, they usually make best growth.

Repton contended, in his Fragments *of 1816, that pointed tree tops (conifers) made the best contrast to formal houses, while the rounded heads of native trees were best suited to the Gothick.*

The Vertical Line

There are occasions and places where a vertical line is an asset. A Wellingtonia, a Redwood or other tall slender conifer will point out, as I have already mentioned, the whereabouts of a great house. The Victorian owner would have planted his treasures near the house (not, as a rule, in the depths of his woodland), where he could watch their progress; a hundred years later, a few tall conifers do indeed add a certain majesty to the curtilage of a dwelling. But away in the landscape such trees look out of place.

Sometimes, particularly where meadows are backed by hills, the slim line of a Lombardy Poplar gives just the punctuation needed in contrast to the rounded forms of native trees, so long as it does not pierce the skyline of trees or hills. The Fastigiate Oak is a suitable alternative for heavy clay and the Dawyck Beech for lighter soils.

The Winter Scene

So far we have been considering trees in their summer dress. Apart from the time of their annual growth, evergreens look much the same in winter or summer. Deciduous trees bring a totally different appearance to the landscape in winter, at which time their bare stems and twigs have a very special value. Their contrast to evergreens, meadow grass, crops and water is so great that in certain winter weather the landscape looks its very best, with far greater variety of colour and texture than in the summer. It is more richly endowed with beauty only in late autumn, when the last yellow leaves on late-shedding trees linger here and there to enliven the colours still more, and in the miracle of spring when certain trees are earlier than others in assuming brilliant green. We can readily absorb all the wonderful variations of the seasons through the year.

In valleys fed by limy streams and rivers, such as in the Cotswolds, and the Test valley near Mottisfont Abbey, we are given the brightest of all winter colours, where the red-twigged willows gleam. There are some incredibly brilliant winter scenes not far from Mottisfont. The orange-brown of the Crack Willow is another notable colour when planted in mass. Poplars mostly provide light putty colour, and the twigs of the ash have the same lightening effect when it is planted in groups in a woodland mainly composed of dark-twigged oak and beech. I need scarcely call attention to the Silver Birch, except to say that with the Common Alder and the beech its twig-colours deepen as the buds start to expand in spring, bringing a purplish tinge. The time was when the English Elm gave that same plum-colour to the days of March, but it will be many decades before we can see this tree again in its massed flowering throughout the country.

The warmest colour among all the native trees and shrubs is provided by the Dogwood common to our limy soils. Its rich red-brown touched with purple in autumn leaf gives way to a thicket of twigs of much the same tone. And because I intend introducing a few exotics for landscape planting this is the place to mention *Cornus alba*, the Red-barked Dogwood from north east Asia. In the summer this Dogwood can easily be taken for a native and it is indeed naturalised in many marshy tracts alongside rivers and lakes. If it can be sited so that the sun shines on it over a sheet of water, with birches and orange-twigged willows nearby, contrasted by some native oaks, hollies and yews, and with the parchment tint of Reed Mace at the water's edge, a grouping of long-lasting winter colour will result that none of summer's bounties can excel. It will all relapse into sober greens during the summer months.

While the colours of greenery are obviously enhanced by direct sunlight, the sun is so much higher in summer that all trees derive some light from its rays. Not so in winter; it is useless to plant trees with coloured twigs to the south of the viewing point, for when seen against the bright light they will merely act as silhouettes.

The Approach to a House

It is quite a difficult job to bear all these things in mind when considering the prospect from a large building – which today may well be a block of flats, a school or institution, or a factory or other major architectural feature. There is the land laid out as in a picture, awaiting the artist's brush to fill in a clump here, a spinney there, open a view or free a flat meadow of a clutter of trees, or adjust fences that level the prospect rather than uplift it. But to get to the building there is often a short or long drive with successive views *across* the parkland, completely at variance with the outlook from the house itself. Sometimes half a dozen views have to be reconciled; it is difficult but not impossible. One easy way out is to plant a spinney so that it shuts out what may be an angle across the principal view from the house. Repton's schemes show the frequent use of this expedient, which carries with it the additional benefit of a sudden clear view and bright light after leaving the spinney. We need be little more concerned than Repton was with the speed of traffic through a private park, but ideas have to be modified and ever larger patches of light and shade provided when we plan to plant near fast-moving traffic along motorways.

"In a park, a road of convenience, and of breadth proportioned to its intention, as an approach to the house for visitors, will often be a circumstance of great beauty." It was Repton who planted the three-mile-long avenue of Common Lime trees at Clumber Park, Nottinghamshire. It is in so large a landscape that it cannot be said to cut it in two from any direction. Because it is so fine a feature a new avenue has been planted so that Clumber can be noted still for its avenue when the first one has eventually to be felled.

3

THE ART OF SCREENING AND PLANTING

Here the grey smooth trunks
Of ash, or lime, or beech, distinctly shine,
Within the twilight of their distant shades;
There lost behind a rising ground, the wood
Seems sunk, and shortened to its topmost boughs.

William Cowper (1731–1800)

Much misguided planting is done under the heading of screening, both in suburban gardens and in the large landscaped spaces, and in every scheme between the two in scope. From the fact that a fastigiate tree concentrates its resources upon growing upright - instead of spreading - follows the other fact that erect trees, planted closely, achieve the object of blotting out the undesirable sights most quickly. While it is perhaps more pleasant for the eye to light on a row of any sort of greenery than on a set of ugly walls, roofs and chimneys, it is equally true to say that nothing calls attention more to the fact that there is something to hide than such a row. It is foreign to the landscape, and therefore cannot really be considered as landscape planting.

On the other hand, there is sometimes too little space available to contemplate any other kind of planting. In built-up areas one's thoughts immediately fly to fast-growing columnar conifers, but unfortunately though they may eschew such things in the broad landscape, planters almost always choose Lombardy Poplars instead. Not only do columnar or fastigiate trees look unnatural, but in time they tend to become bare at the base. The closer they are planted the sooner this happens. In restricted areas there then follows the difficulty of replacement.

Until the coming of the Lawson's Cypress and Western Arborvitae, the Lombardy Poplar was the most popular choice in all positions. Even today this poplar has so got into our system that it is still nearly always the first choice.

The blotting out of nearby buildings in the suburban scene does not really come within the scope of this chapter. A few points are, however, worth

The partly fledged ash tree in the foreground is not thick enough to screen the landscape but increases the perspective. Photographed in Wales.

bringing out because they also apply to the screening of nearby buildings in the landscape. There is no point for instance in planting fast-growing poplars or other trees which achieve great height if the buildings are only about 12 m (40 ft) high. Tall conifers and poplars cannot be topped at such a height and even if such a project were possible the result would be ugly and unsatisfactory, and only temporary. It is better to choose trees which will not greatly exceed 12 m (40 ft); though they may not achieve the object as quickly as we should like they can be interplanted with birch or even poplar for temporary quick effect, as long as a proper programme of thinning or felling is adhered to. Where there is very little space to plant, a scattering of trees of varying heights will, by breaking the view towards the unsightly features, achieve more than a formal wall of greenery. As with other screens it is necessary to think of the ultimate result at the time of planting; all trees tend to become bare below in due course, but this can often be overcome by interplanting with hollies, which will gradually take over their duties even in shade, and reach up to 9 m (30 ft) or more in height.

In the larger landscape there is more scope. A quarter of a mile away a grouping of Lombardy Poplars – preferably not a row – assumes great importance, and is readily permissible on level ground. Such a group is best on its own, not repeated. At Cliveden there are views from the escarpment across hundreds of acres of fields, many of which are outlined with Lombardies, but again this is an unusual feature that is best not repeated. It bears out the old Jekyll-style maxim for garden planting: variation should be within the scheme and not be the scheme itself. This brings us to the most important of principles in landscape planting, that all planting – and particularly screens and shelter belts – should be in accord with the native vegetation or the established planting. In other words, while we may strive after the exotic in our gardens, if we succumb to the temptation to repeat this striving in the landscape we shall tend to shrink the effect and turn it into a garden.

Buildings Attractive and Otherwise

We resort to screening usually when there are unsightly buildings which upset the relative calm of the view or views. There are two qualifications to be borne in mind. One is that a beautiful landscape is brought to life by a touch of human endeavour: a bridge, a curving road, a fence rightly sited, a windmill, a distant church tower or a huddle of houses. The other is that farm buildings, as long as they fit the contours, and are made of (or appear to be made of) traditional materials, are often an asset. It is when roofs – corrugated perhaps – slope in the wrong direction or a lofty dutch barn or silo tower breaks the skyline that irreparable damage is done; or when some rash of new building crops up beyond the confines of the property. Even railways can be amusing, if sufficiently far off and not cluttered with overhead wires, while a new motorway can be a disaster, both to the eye and the ear. Let it be said here and now that only the densest of woods in depth will deaden sound; foliage has little effect.

For shutting out the undesirables we resort to evergreens wherever possible. In the southern half of Britain there is no tree so effective in the long run as the Holm Oak. It is slow-growing, putting on the best growth when exposed to full light; it is therefore useless for planting as an undercrop beneath faster-growing trees. It has the inestimable advantage of retaining its low branches indefinitely, and thus provides a permanent screen from top to browsing line. The answer is to use it wherever possible – on any well-drained land, chalky or otherwise – as a long-term clump, planting behind or in front of it some other quick-growing tree as a temporary measure.

In country where the Scots Pine is already present, on light soil, there is no conifer of greater use and beauty. For chalk or clay the Austrian Pine runs it close, though lacking the tinted stem. The Monterey Pine is quicker and larger than either. A solid phalanx of seed-raised Lawson's Cypress would create a quick screen but would introduce an unfortunate formal feature however planted; the Leyland Cypress is far worse, being completely uniform. *Eucalyptus gunnii* is not to be sneered at; in maturity, at 25 m (80 ft) or so, it conforms to the outlines of our native trees and will I am convinced be accepted eventually as a useful tree for evergreen screens in our warmer counties. The larch, another foreigner, is well known to foresters as a quick crop. If pines or oaks are chosen for the ultimate stand it should be borne in

The foreground – enlivened by shadows, with the trees projecting like the wings on a stage – leads the eye to the distant church at Wiston, West Sussex.

mind that they – and many other trees – become bare-stemmed with age and an initial underplanting of hollies or yews is essential.

The highest, quickest trees are undoubtedly the hybrid poplars (*Populus ×
canadensis* cultivars). When planted in serried ranks they never lose their unblending erect growth, but the Black Italian planted in a group of six to ten trees will create, in the distance, the semblance of a typical park clump of great height. These hybrid trees are collectively the only solution when planting on moist meadows to obscure perhaps an excrescence of buildings on a low hill beyond. There is little need for me to enumerate the rapid screening trees, such as poplar, larch and Douglas Fir; they are well known, although the last should only be used as a temporary measure as it is aesthetically alien to the English landscape. It can, however, be grown for thirty years or so while a long-term screen is maturing.

As a rule these belts and clumps must be surrounded by a fence. Posts and barbed wire can be fairly innocuous at a distance and will frequently be disguised by the growth of brambles, hastened by a planting of thorn. On moist ground, cuttings of Goat Willow put in behind the fence will help to obscure it quickly. But these schemes presuppose an absence of animals.

It is most surprising how many owners of great houses in the past paid no attention to the use of trees as shelter from icy blasts. I call to mind trees which have been planted recently to help keep out the east wind at Gunby Hall, Lincolnshire, and Hatchlands, Surrey, and the buffeting west wind at Peckover House, Cambridgeshire. Sissinghurst Castle garden, in Kent, was always very exposed, particularly from the north and east. Of late years isolated trees coupled with spinneys partly filled with hollies and yews have been planted with an eye to the future. The garden at Trengwainton, Cornwall, was made within a wood of old beeches. These are now falling but over the years belts of evergreen trees, resistant to sea-winds, have been planted outside the beeches and I hope these will be just in time to provide protection when the beeches have all gone. The garden at Uppark, West Sussex, stands on top of the South Downs with an extensive view towards the sea. The view is too grand to obscure, but wings of Holm Oaks have been planted to protect the garden from east and west, and to frame the house.

Tree Guards

One of the most unsightly things in an otherwise idyllic landscape is the tree guard. Bearing in mind that these frequently have to remain for twenty to thirty years it is important that they should be strong and well made. Foresters prefer not to plant single specimens with all the expense it entails but elect instead the small plantation, fenced around, to be thinned perhaps to three or four isolated trees in due course. There is no doubt that trees grow faster in competition, but a few isolated specimens add very much to the broken foreground of tree planting. When an individual tree is put in, it is advisable to plant an attendant screen to hide the tree guard. A small fenced area enclosing perhaps a dozen bushy willows will quickly hide the guard. On drier ground Field Maple or Myrobalan would give the same effect, though more slowly. In many instances it is possible to site the single specimens behind established trees, when the guards will be out of sight. If an old landscape planting is being restored it is seldom possible – or necessary – to place the single trees and small clumps exactly where they were two hundred years ago. Landscape planting is a fluid art and what is an old clump in one decade may have become an open space two decades later; views and plantings come and go.

Repton was often scathing about Brown's plantings in his *Observations*. He realised the difficulty of establishing single trees and goes on to write: "This I apprehend was the origin and intention of those clumps, and that they were never designed as ornaments in themselves, but as the most efficacious and least disgusting manner of producing single trees and groups to vary the surface of a lawn [meadow], and break its uniformity by light and shadow." Also, "In some situations where great masses of wood, and a large expanse of open lawn prevail, the contrast is too violent"; in other words, single trees and small clumps should lead to greater clumps and to the spinneys and woods.

Today's Problems

There are parts of our countryside so denuded of trees that any planting is better than none, and there are waste areas too small for farming and too isolated for building that would benefit by any sort of tree planting. Have we the faith in the future that is needed to do the planting? If so, have we the interest to see that only the most appropriate trees are planted with a definite eye to the embellishment that only the right choice can give? This faith in the future is partly bound up with the age of the planter. At twenty any trees would probably satisfy; the fact that we might watch them growing through the years, overtopping quickly our tiny selves, would in itself give great satisfaction. Few of us, however, look after an estate or garden for fifty years. Even so, if we have faith in beauty, to be planting trees at the age of seventy gives equal pleasure. And I would add that it is possible this book will be used by those who help and advise others to plant, in which case age is of little importance. Fifty years is a long time in anticipation, but short in retrospect. If we know and watch a landscape or a garden for even a quarter of a century our memories and our photographs will quickly prove that we are tending a living work of art, a prospect pulsating with life, and not a static piece of scenery. Nothing is static; old trees decay and fall, opening a new view; young trees shoot up giving new strength to a glade or group; a hedge obscures a special view, or when laid,

West Wycombe Park, Buckinghamshire. Above, an engraving of 1822 by J. & H. S. Storer. Below, a modern photograph of this National Trust property.

opens up a new level; a tree leaning ever outwards darkens a sheet of water, or a lake is invaded by creeping rushes and weeds. Though growth in the main is regulated by the passing seasons no two years are alike and no two have the same effect.

It is not until one has watched natural growth year by year that one begins to understand the meaning of patience and all the good it brings. If we learn this we shall find ourselves looking with equanimity on the apparent slowness of trees, with the same sense of satisfaction as our forbears of the eighteenth century. How hard it must have been for the head gardeners and groundsmen, tending their parterres and avenues, their hedges and topiary, to learn that because Mr Lancelot Brown had made a visit, all was to be swept away and that the cattle were to be encouraged to browse up to the very windows! And that belt after belt and clump after clump of little trees – common native trees – were to be their care for the rest of their working days! Yet this is the frame of mind we need to develop if we are to see the beauty of our countryside re-established. There are those who will quickly grasp what is needed in the way of practical things – fences, posts, seedlings and the like. Repton had to learn these things because he was by nature and partly by upbringing an artist; he began with the grand design. We too should begin with art, so that the practicalities can follow, and if necessary bring adjustments to the scheme.

Having decided that certain fresh plantings or re-plantings are needed, it is advisable to schedule a long-term plan, obviously tackling the most needy section first. Less urgent areas can wait if necessary for some years, and this will have the advantage that woods and groves will not all be at the same stage of growth in, say, fifty years, nor for that matter in old age. There is also the question of tree surgery; it is expensive but it certainly prolongs the life of some picturesque old trees, especially oaks and Sweet Chestnuts. There is not only picturesqueness to be considered, but also, if the area is open to the public, the danger of falling branches from untended trees.

Problems and Solutions

Repton was very skilful with his pencil and brush. His drawings usually depict the scene as it is on an attached flap, with his suggested improvements underneath. It is an admirable adjunct to plan-drawing, but it is not a substitute. Today we should probably take a monochrome photograph, enlarge it considerably and then paint in upon a slide or flap what the proposed planting might look like in, say, fifty years. The photograph and sketch are much more convincing than a plan. A quicker, on-the-spot, method which I have often employed is a rapid pencil sketch, roughly in perspective, with a red-ink sketch superimposed to show fresh planting at its maturity.

Selworthy, Somerset, a National Trust property. A sketch by Peter Richard Hoare, c. 1820. In the dramatic terrain the tree shapes, including Lombardy Poplars, are shown but do not confuse the lines of the hills. This pen-and-wash work was a quick method of depiction before the advent of the camera.

Some years ago I met an owner of a fair-sized garden and landscape who was a considerable landscape artist in oils. I noticed that she had done several paintings of the garden and landscape to the south, north and east but none to the west, despite the fact that in this direction was a sheet of water in front of rising ground. I was not there to advise on the landscape, but on the garden. However, my curiosity was aroused and a question brought the answer that the wood on top of the slight hill spoilt the view. I suggested she might paint the landscape as she would like it and let me see it. This she did and it resulted in an extension of the wood flowing down the hillside just as Repton would have ordained! It is by such simple means that one can determine what should be done. The mind quickly glosses over the long interim of gradual growth. Her scheme reminded me of Robert Louis Stevenson: "The hills about Wendover, and, as far as I could see, all the hills in Buckinghamshire, wear a sort of hood of beech plantation; but in this particular case the hood had been suffered to extend itself into something more like a cloak and hung down about the shoulders of the hill in wide folds, instead of lying flatly along the summit."

Apart from the general gradual wastage through gales and old age we are sometimes suddenly confronted by a complete change of landscape – if a neighbouring landowner fells a wood, for instance, or if one's treescape has been composed entirely of elm. At Penrhyn Castle, Gwynedd, the sheltered walled garden became open to the north through the clear-felling of a wood on the estate, while at Lytes Cary, Somerset, the surrounding land within a year or two became a spectral landscape filled with hundreds of dead elms.

Another such instance of elm disease opened the entire perimeter of some school playing fields to the view of rows of houses of a fair height. It was resolved to have a new evergreen screen planted regardless of the masses of elm suckers that were arising; we do not know how long it will be before these too suffer a like fate. There was fortunately space for more than just a few rows of cypresses. The solution in the long term was an alternating planting of Holm Oaks and Austrian Pines. The site was well drained and open. Holm Oaks remain clothed to the ground where there are no cattle, but of course take long to mature, and so behind them was a massed planting of birches. The Austrian Pines, because in time they become bare below, were interplanted with hollies and yews and backed by a few birches. If all goes well, this planting should result in an evergreen screen for a hundred years or more and avoid excessive height which is not necessary because of the moderate height of the neighbouring buildings. In the foreground was a mixed assembly of shrubs with light foliage.

The bare Clee Hills of Shropshire stand above the rising ground in the middle distance capped by Stanway Coppice (National Trust). A few trees planted in the two short lengths of hedges which run up the field slope would help to link the coppice with the trees in the valley.

The problem at Attingham was quite different. Here, across a flat meadow, is a spinney of deciduous trees, a wall, a main road (the A5) and a distant prospect of the Shropshire hills. Repton did a Red Book for Attingham Park, and his original scheme has largely been repeated, but he concerned himself little with the distant view. In recent years, to create a more pleasing and varied prospect from the portico of the house some foreground trees of large size have been introduced, adding perspective and allowing the eye to follow through to the highest points of the hills. The spinney has been underplanted with hollies and yews, which will be quite tall enough in the future to shut out the glint of vehicles on the road which bounds the park on this side. A few deciduous trees will still be encouraged to break the long line of evergreens, but not where the hills dominate.

Early Inspection and Advice

I mentioned earlier that "time" is of great importance – time to assess the possibilities of a site and time for growth to begin and mature. There is also the importance of the timing of the first advisory visit especially on sites that are being "developed", where it is necessary that every care should be taken of established trees *from the start*. Protection of branches and roots and the level of the surrounding ground are all vital to the embellishment of the

From the Attingham Park Red Book by Repton, 1797. On the right, his proposed improvements in the treatment of the marshy River Tern and in tree planting. A property of the National Trust.

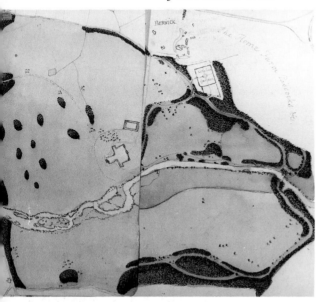
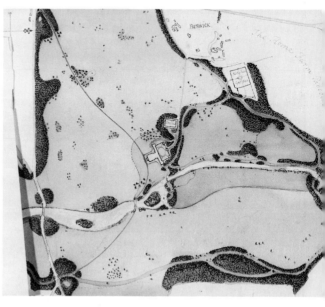

76

The view across the park from the portico at Attingham, Shropshire (National Trust). The main road, the A5, runs along the walled boundary of the park just beyond the spinney of trees, which at present obscures the view of the distant hills. Below, by underplanting the spinney with hollies (vertical hatching) a lower evergreen screen will be achieved and, as the trees fall, views to the hills will open. Clumps and single trees in the foreground and middle distance will increase the perspective as they grow to maturity.

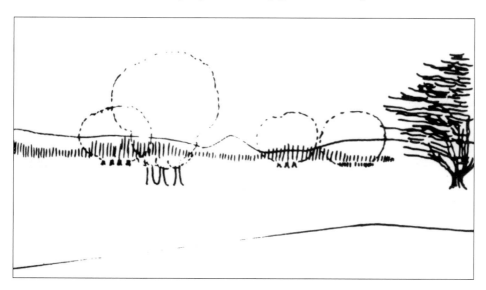

site in its immediate and distant future. This early attention to the safety of trees is something that should be advised upon and ensured by the landscape gardener on the first visit. It is unfortunate that architects and builders, to say nothing of owners, often postpone calling in the gardener until all sorts of horrors have been perpetrated. The siting of the building, of the drive, of the very terrace and garden and all that belongs to it may well have been decided before consultation. Once ground is in an unmentionable state, the garden designer is summoned for advice on what to plant. Ideally the first consideration should surely be for the gardener to plot and examine all trees and shrubs on the site; to recommend any treatment necessary, to preserve all that are worthy from branch and root damage and compaction of the soil, and to discuss with the architect the general layout, the light, the background and the need, if any, for screening.

Naturalised Plants

If a crop of any kind is being taken off the ground – trees or herbs – it is practically impossible to foster the native flora, except for plants which will grow on the semi-woodland floor and in meadows where the first hay-cut or grazing occurs late enough for plants to set seed. But steep banks, ditches and hedgerows still provide footholds for many British natives.

There are, however, certainly two and perhaps three bulbous plants which we all enjoy which will grow to perfection in thin woodland and one, our native daffodil, the Lent Lily, *Narcissus pseudonarcissus*, which can also be used to enliven March meadows. Apart from the Pheasant Eye Narcissus, to which I shall refer later, the Lent Lily is the only daffodil which can be naturalised in the open field or thin woodland. Its main qualification is that it is a genuine native but it also reproduces itself quickly from seed and thus achieves that desirable slight variation in the opening and the quality of the flowers. In Wales *N. obvallaris*, the Welsh Daffodil, might be preferred, but in my experience it does not seed itself, at least in the garden, though it is difficult to believe seeds are not produced in the wild. It is a taller plant and a brighter yellow than the Lent Lily. One of the last species of *Narcissus* to flower, *N. poeticus recurvus*, the Late Pheasant Eye, coupled perhaps with *N. ornatus*, the Early Pheasant Eye, are both permissible for naturalising. They are white, and the former flowers with the native Bluebell *Endymion non-scriptus* (*Scilla nutans*), in early May. These make a pleasant grouping when grown together. The one thing to avoid for naturalising is the "naturalising mixture" of daffodils. Not only do such mixtures usually contain some hideous doubles and garish varieties with orange trumpets or cups, but they also stay where they are planted, waxing into ever denser clumps and not spreading by seeds to any appreciable extent. They and all the named kith and kin are to be avoided for naturalising in the landscape – whatever may be permitted within gardens and the immediate surrounds of a dwelling. I deplore the planting of "grandiflora" garden daffodils on country road verges, however appropriate they may be in towns and villages, modern parks and other man-made environments.

The Lent Lily is difficult to buy; even if bulb merchants accept orders, the true species is seldom supplied. Eschewing all garden daffodils means that there will be a month's pause between the Lent Lily (apart from the Early Pheasant Eye, not often seen naturalised) and bluebell time. But perhaps this is just as well; plenty of daffodils will be in flower in gardens.

All these bulbs are very adaptable to light or heavy soils, but do not take kindly to hungry chalk or boggy clay. They can be planted as dry bulbs in autumn, or immediately after flowering, with the leaves left on. Since the Lent Lily and the bluebell seed so freely, they may be sown *in situ* from seeds, but in any case even a scattered planting may well become a sheet of blossom in twenty years. The Wood Anemone, *Anemone nemorosa*, is another charmer for thin woodland.

Man-made Sites

I have left until last the consideration of the most difficult of all projects – the reinstatement of sites of industrial waste. The Forestry Commission published in 1979 *Tree Planting on Man-made Sites in Wales* by K. F. Broad. This is a publication of immense importance to all those who are confronted by this daunting task. The pros and cons are fully set out from an almost entirely practical point of view and some wonderful results have been achieved. Reptonian niceties cannot always be considered; the priority is to find out what will grow on spoil heaps and to get it growing as soon as possible. Greenery is the main thing; after that comes the improvement of the "soil" and the microclimate, which is a long-term project.

Here it is worth recording that in addition to plants and trees of the Legume family – which accumulate nitrogen from the air in their root-nodules through bacteria and thus enrich the soil – the alders have a similar beneficial effect in producing nitrogen through the action of fungi. (The same is true of the Sea Buckthorn, *Hippophaë rhamnoides*, which is a useful colonising shrub for dry or wet soils of a sandy nature.) The value of the alders, particularly *Alnus glutinosa*, *A. incana* and *A. rubra*, which thrive even on spoil-heaps on windy sites that would barely support other trees, is thus increased still further.

On some sites there are greater opportunities for experiment and artistry than on others. Whatever the problems, I believe the essentials are the consideration of the whole from an ideal, aesthetic point of view, and the adaptation of that ideal to whatever is practicable. While the fundamental is the provision of greenery, wherever possible it should be varied within the theme, and with these basic thoughts I will leave this invaluable work to those who have first-hand knowledge of it. But Repton's ideals remain the same wherever we may work.

4

PRACTICAL POINTS IN REGARD TO PLANTING

They lighted down in a fair thick wood, which did entice them
with the pleasantness of it to take their rest there. It was all of pine
trees, whose broad heads, meeting together yielded a perfect shade
to the ground, where their bodies gave a spacious and pleasant
room to walk in.

Sir Philip Sidney (1554–86)

The choice of trees is governed by many different but related things, and
the whole matter is subservient to the use to which the land is to be put.
Next comes the consideration, and perhaps the testing, of the soil, and the
question of drainage. Though many trees will eventually succeed on dry
slopes there are few which thrive in ill-drained meadows. In general the soil
in Britain is of what is called "normal fertility" – in which category we may
include a wide variety of soils, with such extreme examples as almost pure
sand or chalk, or a shallow rough medium over broken stones, deep alluvial
peats and their relatives, or pure boggy clay. It is amazing that the tree-
planter need never despair; species can be found to thrive in all these
circumstances.

Local Conditions

Rainfall in Britain varies considerably from light, perhaps 50 cm (20 in) per
year, in the south-east to double that or more in the west and north-west.
These variations have to be taken into account. Deciduous trees can be
planted at any time during autumn and winter, while the ground is open
and in fit condition; evergreens are best planted in early autumn or spring,
when the soil is warm. At whatever time during the winter the trees are
planted, they seldom make much or indeed any root until about the middle
of March. All planters long for those idyllic April weeks when there is
warm sunshine, and soft south-westerlies bring showers. Unfortunately
April is a capricious month and is just as likely to be dry and cold, often into

May. It stands to reason therefore that in the drier parts of the country, the new trees, deciduous or evergreen, should be in their places by the end of February or early March. No amount of care taken to keep the roots moist during planting is wasted. A trap for the unwary is the healing in of bundles of seedlings on arrival from nurseries: the bundles should be opened and the seedlings "lined out" so that each one's roots are in contact with soil.

When warm moist weather does come, the weeds will grow as fast as the trees and some sort of cleaning, by hand, or by weedkiller using an Arborguard, is advisable; no young trees like to be throttled by weeds and grass tufts and when the summer's first really hot spells come, in June, the testing time arrives. If they can survive into August, when nights lengthen and dews increase, all will usually be well. Some failures will no doubt still occur and cause further work in patching the following year.

Local Scenery

Having ascertained the state of the soil and climate, we have next to consider the general scenery and observe what trees grow well in the different areas and levels. It is always safest to let our choice of species be swayed by what is already growing. Just to illustrate a few extremes, we can hardly go wrong with beech on chalk, Hornbeam and oak on heavy soils, Sweet Chestnut, birch and pine on sand, Sycamore and ash on windswept rocky uplands, and willows and poplars for moist ground. This does not of course mean that these trees will not all thrive in our soils "of normal fertility". It is obvious that the oak, Britain's commonest tree, flourishes on a great variety of soils.

The biggest visual difference is between conifers and broad-leafed trees. There is no doubt that some of the severe outlines of acres of quick-growing conifers planted in its early days by the Forestry Commission and other owners caused offence. Today there is more tolerance towards the broad-leafed trees and it has been found that mixed woodland, or areas of conifers intermingled with areas of native hardwoods, gives aesthetically the best result, improves the soil to a greater degree than where conifers are exclusively planted and minimises the depredation of pests and the incidence of disease. There is no doubt that conifers in the mass are monotonously dark but they are quick producers of timber and used with circumspection can enhance a landscape, provided that an irregular planting of hardwoods offers occasional relief. Though denied being natives of this country by the shifting of continents and the Ice Age, they are obviously very much at home in our areas of highest rainfall and are still to be seen achieving an ever greater height. Their height is the main disadvantage aesthetically as I have been at pains to stress earlier in this book.

As mentioned earlier this is not a book about afforestation; however, it should be said that in wide landscapes, whether undulating or mountainous, particularly in the west and north, the mass planting of trees for profit can hardly be turned down on grounds of pure aesthetics. Fortunately, after she had retired as Landscape Consultant to the Forestry Commission, Dame Sylvia Crowe recorded her thoughts and unique experience of this great work in *The Landscape of Forests and Woods*. In his foreword, Mr John Mackie, Chairman of the Commission, recorded that her principles have been adopted as the Commission's policy on landscape design. The booklet is fully illustrated with colour photographs, together with revealing diagrams which call attention to the important landscape features and show how sensitive planting can emphasise them, and at the same time provide plenty of opportunity for forest planting on land that is perhaps not fit for anything else. Having studied the pictures and diagrams it would be difficult for anyone to write off conifers as contributors to the beauty of the landscape. There are some pictures showing the worst that has happened in block-planting with straight rides and sides. There are many others showing how, by the subtle mixing of evergreen conifers with larch and native broad-leaves, the undulations of the terrain can be preserved and indeed enhanced. I think this thoughtful booklet will do as much for the beauty of the great expanses of the land as I hope the Reptonian ideas I am setting forth may do for the more limited parkland.

Desired Height

In selecting the best kind of tree to fit into the scenery, we should also consider the desired height of the tree in maturity. There is no point, for instance, in planting a screen of beech and oak, or any other tree likely to reach between 18 m (60 ft) and 30 m (100 ft), if the same benefit would accrue from a belt of Field Maple or Crack Willow which will remain bushy. It is the choice of species that will lend enchantment to the landscape, in form and colour in winter or summer, and when seen against the light or with the light mainly shining on them.

Other points to be considered are the accentuation of natural features, and the choice of background to important features such as buildings. Scale, likewise, in relation to the landscape and buildings should be another priority. When planting near to buildings we have to take account of the safety factor, which in turn is governed by light and branches, roots and soil. Clay subsoils suggest what we may plant but they are very liable to shrinkage in dry weather, causing subsequent damage to buildings. This is aggravated by "thirsty" types of trees such as poplars, willows and ash. Probably 30 m (100 ft) is the nearest that big trees should be planted to buildings.

These two pictures from Repton's Observations, 1805, show several points. If well-grown standard trees are planted, suitably spaced, the result is vertical stems; if seedlings are planted irregularly placed, trees will develop a natural lean. Clumps of trees planted in open ground do not govern the view as others do when fenced and underplanted with bushes.

Planting Sizes

The choice of size of stock for planting is easily made. The smallest available, compatible with easy handling, are always the best: they are cheapest (and thus the cost will be less for any replacements needed); they catch hold of the soil quickly, partly because they are young and have not been unduly disturbed, and partly because they will, when planted firmly, be more proof against wind-rocking; in addition they will not need staking if they are less than 60 cm (2 ft) in height.

Mixed Plantings

A glance at established mixed woodland, where trees have seeded themselves over the last hundred years or so, will reveal that there is a general pattern and that trees tend to grow best where they are best suited, which is as might be expected. The species do not occur in separate blocks, but overlap and mingle with one another. An acre of oaks might thin out to beeches on one side and to ash trees on the other, and a few oaks would spill over among the beeches, likewise among the ash trees. Furthermore the trees will not be equally spaced. The forester likes to plant his seedlings in rows, which certainly makes care easier during the first three years or so. Subsequent thinning will *help* to destroy the effect of regimentation, but nothing achieves this better than putting in an extra tree here and there among the rows. Perhaps this might be thought a waste of time, but Repton in his *Observations* wrote, "No groups will appear natural unless two or more trees are planted very near to each other ... and of different age, size, and character." Undoubtedly this is of prime importance in planting small clumps, rather than in woodlands. Repton even recommended planting two trees of different species in the same hole to achieve his aim.

Protection of Trees

There remain the bigger specimens in the foreground to be considered in relation to the perspective of the view. Here we may be allowed to plant large trees, in separate guards. The guards will cost perhaps ten times as much as the trees but are essential if cattle or horses are used as "mowers". Because guards are so costly it is best to spare nothing to make them strong and long-lasting. The young tree needs a tall stake inserted at the time of planting so that the leader can be trained up in aftercare. The top of the guard has to be so high and wide that animals cannot catch hold of side branches and tear them down and off. Often, in spite of great care, the animals win. This is why it is usually thought preferable to plant small clumps, fenced around securely, with the object of thinning to one or two trees in, say, twenty years' time. All guards, fences and ties should be kept under constant supervision and it is best to provide for access to make the use of weedkiller possible for the first five years. If the young trees have to be protected against sheep only, the animals will do most of the necessary cleaning. On poor land it may be advisable to use weedkiller around the young trees as a preliminary to applying fertiliser.

It is of course essential that protection should go hand in hand with planting. Rabbits and hares quickly play havoc with little trees, evergreen or deciduous, particularly if snow is on the ground. Protection is as much a professional job as planting and it is best to take local advice on the matter. It is an expensive business; the high cost of wire netting has undoubtedly been responsible for some of the straight-sided belts and clumps that upset the landscape. So much depends upon what they are being guarded against – every living creature seems to be against them, whether it is horses, cattle, deer, sheep, hares, rabbits, or just hooligans. Fortunately all these are seldom combined in one area. Spiral PVC guards are proof against rabbits, hares and sheep. Though black PVC is the least noticeable, in sunny counties it has been known to damage the bark by the heat generated in hot weather. Sleeves of plastic netting can be used against deer, up to a considerable height. Cattle and horses are a great trouble because of their weighty bulk and long necks. The Countryside Commission's *Tree Guards (Management and Design Notes No. 6)*, compiled by Paul Walshe and Christopher West-lake, gives an admirable survey of all the difficulties and remedies in metal, wood, wire and plastics, and should be in the hands of all intending planters.

The most effective barrier against hooligans is a row of Sweet Brier (*Rosa rubiginosa, R. eglanteria*). This forms a beautiful hedge without clipping and thrives on any reasonable soil in full light. I have sometimes used it for temporary interplanting between laurels, hollies and yews; the evergreens in due course smother the briers. There are some places where barbed wire is too obvious and unsightly; used in conjunction with Sweet Brier, a well-nigh impenetrable thicket can be achieved which still looks like a piece of natural planting.

Hedgerow Trees

If we are to reinstate hedgerow trees due care in their selection is necessary. Beech and chestnuts make dense, wide heads, which will not encourage any kind of crop, but oak and ash, and perhaps Sycamore, are more suitable. The elms likewise have been used much in the past in hedgerows.

New Roads

For several decades past, the countryside has been periodically sliced into unrelated pieces by new roads. Sometimes the road goes through woodland or clumps of trees which are felled as necessary, leaving trees of upright, thin quality at the new end of the belt. In the interest of the beauty of the landscape it is vital to fell a few more so that only good, branched trees meet the eye, and to make possible the planting of young trees to heal the denuded portions. Some portions of the land to the side of new embanked roads may become waterlogged or a pond may even be formed. Every chance should be taken to turn any unwanted sites such as these into conservation areas.

The Value of Instant Recognition

Sometimes I take a party of students into the country and get them to study trees in the distance, naming at least the genus if not the species. All recognise a Lombardy Poplar or a Weeping Willow, but when it comes to distinguishing at a quarter or half a mile an oak or beech, an elm or ash, it is a different matter. Botanists among them could readily tell me the difference in the leaf or bark. But instant long-range recognition is highly important for two reasons: training the eye to the general outline of the different species is a pleasant enough exercise in itself, but it also brings home to the student that he or she is searching for character which will have importance in an imaginary landscape. In other words, by studying trees at a distance the mind's eye is learning to gauge their value in relation to one another.

The imagination is very much to the fore in landscape planting. After some years of thought and experiment we can visualise the general effect of, for instance, an oak, and how, whether isolated or in woodland, it will appear in different lights at different times of the year. The fact that it can be recognised instantly in the distance proves that the mind's eye has observed its value in the landscape.

The mind's eye also has a slight tendency towards wishful thinking. In visualising a tree we do not think of it in adolescence or in a decaying condition, but rather in its splendid maturity. This may be only about a third of its life; there is, however, much to be gained by contemplating a tree when it is young and growing fast, and equally there is no doubt that our landscape would be the poorer if all trees were felled at their prime. Owls and other birds and a vast number of insects favour a decaying tree.

Seed-raised Plants

Our native trees are comparatively few in number and within each species there is a great range of different growth and shape. This is what makes distant recognition tricky, but exciting. After hundreds of generations our trees have not developed into pure strains, though good and bad stands may be detected. These are mostly due, however, not to generations of self-selection, but to being in ideal conditions. Much has been learnt by foresters about seed-strains of quick-growing conifers in regard to our climate, the production of timber and resistance to disease. In order to extract the utmost from crops of timber, people may be tempted at some future stage to develop pure seed-strains, just as we do for farming crops. If this happened, their vulnerability to destruction by pests and diseases would be increased. A more worrying thought is that, still with an eye on timber profits, the time may come when the vegetative reproduction (instead of seed-raising) of broad-leafed trees is contemplated. This is perhaps not so remote a prospect when we consider the strides made in the vegetative propagation of nursery stock during the last few decades. Then should we see not only uniformity in conifer afforestation, but among broad-leafed trees as well. It would be the death knell of the sort of scheme I am putting forward in this book. What is desirable in an avenue or a hedge - complete uniformity - is

For landscape planting it is almost essential to use seed-raised stock, to avoid uniformity. These three Spanish or Sweet Chestnuts at Mottisfont Abbey, Hampshire (National Trust), show considerable variety of habit in the one species.

not desirable in woodland or in isolated trees in our landscape. We may bless *Chamaecyparis lawsoniana* 'Green Hedger' because of its uniformity in a hedge – or a clone of English Yew or a holly vegetatively propagated in a similar way – but for informal planting seed-raised stock is preferable.

The beauty of our woods, spinneys and clumps is due to the fact that they are composed of individuals, each one different from the next. The fact that some of them may be "runts" or even hybrids matters not in the least. In an arboretum we need to know the history of each particular specimen but in woodlands this is of no importance.

In our landscape planting, therefore, we should only contemplate the purchase of seed-raised trees and shrubs. The variation is there to delight the eye, as it is in thorn trees which are always raised from seed; the Guelder Rose and other natives are as often as not propagated from cuttings in a nursery. A belt of Guelder Rose of exact uniformity would not lend the enchantment to the scene that would be given by individual seedlings. This is of course why the seed-raised Pontic Rhododendron is of such supreme value in the landscape; every plant is different and flowers a few days before or after the next, creating a blend rather than a blare.

Sometimes, when I encounter a group of garden design students, I find they tend to speak of trees, shrubs and plants either as "soft material" (as opposed to gravel, brick, stone, concrete or timber) or – which I think is even worse – "plant material". These terms not only use two words instead of one, but either of them relegates plants to a secondary position in the order of things. It is conveniently forgotten that without plants there would be no garden design, no landscape planting.

Let us then, in the next chapter, discuss the values not of the "plant material", but of the plants themselves, the ingredients of our landscape palette.

5

A LIST OF TREES AND SHRUBS
for Landscape Planting
and for Temporary Screening

The green trees when I saw them first through one of the gates
transported and ravished me, their sweetness and unusual beauty
made my heart to leap, and almost mad with ecstasy, they were
such strange and wonderful things.

Thomas Traherne (1636–74)

In the following descriptions of trees and shrubs at our disposal I have
adopted modern nomenclature but have added synonyms where they are,
or have been in common usage, as well as the vernacular names where
available. The scale of heights should be read with considerable reservation;
growth varies greatly in different conditions and some of the foreign trees
have not yet been in cultivation long enough in Britain for them to have
achieved their full height. The heights given must therefore be accepted as
approximate and represent what we find in general throughout the country,
in gardens or countryside. Greater heights will be attained in areas where
growth is exceptional. The plant's character is also indicated, with (D) for
deciduous and (E) for evergreen. It will be noted that, although most plants
are native to this country, I have included some foreigners or hybrids, for
instance, where they have long been accepted in our landscapes (cedar,
Holm Oak); for quick screening (*Eucalyptus*, hybrid poplars, larch); for
medium height because natives are scarce (some each of *Prunus*, *Salix*,
Sorbus); and for evergreen underplanting (laurel, *Rhododendron*, privet).
There are also the immensely tall foreign conifers, but I think I have sounded
enough warnings about these. The choice is between informal and formal
trees, though the Lombardy Poplar is an exception.

Foreign trees, however "accepted" they have become in the landscape,
should be used with restraint and this applies particularly to the following:
Cedrus, *Cupressus macrocarpa*, *Larix*, *Nothofagus*, *Platanus*, Weeping Willows,
Tilia × *petiolaris* and *T. tomentosa*. Others are included in the list simply
because they have some special value in screening as opposed to landscape
planting.

The colour and pattern of the bark of trees in winter is no less distinctive than the tint of their twigs. An old Sweet or Spanish Chestnut, left, at Killerton, Devon (National Trust), and a Black Italian Poplar in the University Botanic Garden, Cambridge.

In every instance I have tried to draw attention to the most important points regarding the effect of the plants both near at hand and far away: these are the points of most value for our purpose. Though I have also given some details of flowers and fruit these in the main add little to the tree's effect in the landscape. Preferences of soil and conditions have been mentioned where the plants' tolerance is limited.

The species comprise approximately the following scale of sizes: deciduous, 26 tall, 23 medium, 20 short; evergreens, 12 tall, 8 short. In addition there are the conifers. Enough all told, I think, to provide ample variation for our landscapes.

Our native trees and their characteristics have been treated in innumerable books in the past and it might be thought that there was nothing more to be said about them. They have been the subject of folklore and history, of botanical study and forestry assessments. But I venture to suggest that my list, instead of covering these aspects, singles out a new one, by indicating what the plants may do for us in the landscape. In short, it is a list for the landscape gardener. While bearing in mind William Robinson's notable contributions in something like the same approach, I believe this is the first time such an attempt has been made.

As Hilaire Belloc wrote:

"This forest is like a thing so changeful of its nature that change clings to it as a quality, apparent even during the glance of a moment. This forest makes a picture which is designed, but not seizable. It is a scheme, but a scheme you cannot set down. It is of those things which can best be retained by mere copying with a pencil or a brush. It is of those things which a man cannot fully receive, and which he cannot fully re-express to other men."

Abies   Silver Fir

Species	D/E*	Approx. Height	Native Habitat	Date of Introduction
A. alba (A. pectinata) European Silver Fir	E	30–45 m 100–150 ft	Central and S. Europe	c. 1680
A. procera (A. nobilis) Noble Fir	E	30–37 m 100–120 ft	Western USA	1831
A. grandis Giant Fir	E	30–45 m 100–150 ft	Western USA	c. 1832

* Deciduous or evergreen

Species of *Abies* give a prim soldierly appearance and are foreign to our landscapes. The European Silver Fir was much planted during the nineteenth century and today pokes out of established woodland in a scraggy and unattractive way. The Noble Fir is a considerable improvement and *A. grandis* is one of the fastest-growing conifers. There are many more such foreigners which succeed in our climate, but are only suited to the arboretum and large garden and not the landscape into which they never fit sympathetically.

ACER   Maple

Species	D/E	Approx. Height	Native Habitat	Date of Introduction
A. campestre Field Maple	D	9–15 m 30–50 ft or more	Europe (Britain), Near East, Africa	
A. pseudoplatanus Sycamore ('Plane' in Scotland)	D	21–30 m 70–100 ft	Europe	Long ago
A. platanoides Norway or Norwegian Maple	D	18–21 m 60–70 ft	Europe south of Norway, not Britain	Late 17th cent.
A. negundo Box Elder	D	6–12 m 20–40 ft	N. America	1688

The Field Maple is one of the few natives which grow only to medium size; trees over 15 m (50 ft) are exceptional, though some may be seen at Sizergh Castle, Cumbria. In spite of this it is vigorous as a youngster, of great beauty in its coppery tinted young foliage and again in autumn when yellow and red predominate. Old trees are more or less static, growing very slowly, and make old-looking rugged specimens. The flowers are not conspicuous. It prefers calcareous soils, will grow well on chalk or heavy land and its great value is for furnishing the fringes of belts and for use in isolation in hedgerows.

The Sycamore on the other hand is by now one of the commonest trees in the country, particularly on waste land which it will quickly colonise from trees nearby. Having been introduced, it is thought, in Roman times, it has established itself as a native throughout England, South Scotland and Wales, but is rare in Ireland. Owners of exposed upland farms on stony ground in the north of England, and in Wales and Scotland, have reason to bless it. It is early to leaf, often showing bronzy tints, after which the beautiful nodding racemes of yellowish flowers appear. For the summer it is an undistinguished green, changing to yellow in autumn, before which the bunches of "keys" turn to greenish red. Extremely fast-growing when young, it settles down after fifty years or so into a densely branched rounded head. For our purpose it is useful as a rapid temporary screen; in poor, hilly sites it is invaluable. In spite of its weedy nature, nobody can deny the majesty of a fine old specimen, such as we not infrequently see particularly in Devon (at Saltram Park, for instance), and in Yorkshire and Wales. It is specially valuable in maritime districts as it will withstand salt-laden winds.

It is thus often the first tree of any size – though maybe stunted and bent – in a shore plantation. It will thrive in any normal soil.

The Norwegian Maple can be confused with the Sycamore at first sight, but has a brilliance in spring unsurpassed at that time – from its bunches of yellow-green flowers before the leaves appear. The leaves are smoother and of a fresher green, and in autumn turn to brilliant tints, mostly yellow. This European tree was brought to Britain in the late seventeenth century and is raised from seeds, which frequently germinate spontaneously, anywhere. It is thus useful for landscape planting as it adds colour twice a year without appearing to be a foreigner. It grows best in good soils, but is not particular, and rapidly gives results, making a medium-sized, dome-like head in maturity. Including it here and there in the fringes of plantations a pleasing diversion is assured and it blends into the general canopy. Even earlier to flower is the smaller *A. opalus*.

The silly name of "Box Elder" (since it has no relationship to box or to elder) was almost enough to make me exclude this foreigner, but we are not over-endowed with plain green trees of this size. Its green is light in tone, turning to yellow in autumn. The winter twigs are a good green. With its pleasant colours and useful size it has quite a lot to recommend it and it grows happily in any normal soil.

AESCULUS   Horse Chestnut

Species	D/E	Approx. Height	Native Habitat	Date of Introduction
A. hippocastanum Horse Chestnut	D	18–30 m 60–100 ft	N. Greece and Albania	early 17th cent.
A.h. 'Baumannii' (*A.h. flore pleno*)	D	18–30 m 60–100 ft	Alsace	c. 1820

The "conker tree" is known by everyone. It is a native of Eastern Europe and was introduced in the early seventeenth century. Because of its prolificity and ability to sow itself it is found everywhere and is looked upon as a native. It thrives in any soil but does best in sheltered positions on account of its heavy branching habit, being particularly suited to moist meadows. Its merits as a landscape tree are its contendedness with rather wet conditions and also its low branches, which when retained in grazing land give a particularly neat and dense browsing line. Where browsing results in something unsightly being seen, its value for planting in less well-drained hollows will result in the browsing line being lowered, thus giving better screening. Its early leafing is also valuable for screening and its flamboyance at flowering time is well known. In autumn it presents a variety of brilliant tints.

93

Dense conifers at Chipping Campden, Gloucestershire, will soon obscure the church. The narrow outline of lime trees leads the eye to the dominant cumulous masses of Horse Chestnuts.

There are many good specimens about the country but I know of few better than those at Powis Castle, Powys. Like the Common Ash its silhouette in winter is specially good, but unlike that tree its appearance in summer is solid, dark and lumpy; it is likely to be the most solid and heavy of all trees when used near to the eye. Its very dark bark – both trunk and twigs – in winter adds to the varied tints of woodlands, where, drawn up by neighbours, it will develop lofty boles. It is one of the quickest growers when young. In places where conker-seekers need to be discouraged, the double-flowered form 'Baumannii' should be chosen as it is sterile. The various species of *Aesculus* and hybrids with flowers of pink or other tints do not blend into the landscape, nor are they of such majestic growth.

ALNUS   Alder

Species	D/E	Approx. Height	Native Habitat	Date of Introduction
A. glutinosa Common Alder	D	15–21 m 50–70 ft	Europe (Britain), W. Asia, N. Africa	
A. incana Grey Alder	D	15–18 m 50–60 ft	Europe and the the Caucasus	1780
A. rubra Red Alder	D	12–18 m 40–60 ft	Western N. America	1880
A. cordata Italian Alder	D	18–25 m 60–80 ft	Corsica and S. Italy	c. 1820

The alders are not spectacular trees but have great value because they thrive in wet cold places, like willows. Unlike willows they are comparatively dark and almost formal in appearance. This is particularly true of the Common Alder, whose dark bark and twigs are echoed by brownish male catkins in spring followed by small, almost black cones from the female catkins which last through the winter. Late spring is its great moment when the purplish buds swell accompanied by the lengthening catkins; at that season it rivals the birch in rich colouring. With its very dark green foliage it makes a strong contrast to willows through winter and summer.

My reason for including three foreign species is not only that they give the appearance of natives, but that they thrive in untoward situations. The Grey Alder, whose twigs are greyish, not purplish, is invaluable for planting on slag heaps and in similar poor, windswept positions, wet or dry. Few trees of middle height equal these species' ability to thrive in conditions unconducive to normal tree growth; the Red Alder is specially resistant to wind. Both the Grey and the Red have conspicuous yellow catkins in spring and dark green summer foliage. The Italian Alder is a tree of some character, of narrow and rather conical outline. It retains its dark green glossy foliage until early winter, after which the cones are conspicuous, though the spring catkins are less showy than those of the others. It is of rapid growth on almost any soil, including chalk.

All alders blend perfectly with our native trees, and those with a penchant for the genus would do well to consider the Japanese *A. firma* with its beautiful hornbeam-like leaves and the Himalayan *A. nitida* whose catkins appear in autumn.

AMELANCHIER Serviceberry

Species	D/E	Approx. Height	Native Habitat	Date of Introduction
A. ovalis Snowy Mespilus	D	3–4.5 m 10–15 ft	Central and S. Europe	1596
A. laevis	D	3–5.5 m 10–18 ft	Eastern N. America	1780

The second species has hybridised and a whole range of types are found on Surrey commons, from which it may be deduced that they are admirably suited to acid, sandy and dry soils. *A. lamarckii*, *A. × grandiflora* or *A. confusa* are names sometimes used for these hybrids. All make small trees or free-growing large open shrubs, beautiful in spring with tinted young foliage and white flowers, and have good autumn colour. They like open sunny positions.

BETULA   Birch

Species	D/E	Approx. Height	Native Habitat	Date of Introduction
B. pendula (*B. verrucosa*) Silver Birch	D	12–18 m 40–60 ft	Europe (Britain), N. Asia	
B. pubescens (*B. alba* in part) Downy Birch	D	12–18 m 40–60 ft	Europe (Britain), N. Asia	

The Silver Birch with its white stems has a particular place in our landscapes; no other tree gives so much lightness and grace. Botanists have long argued over the two kinds native to Britain and it is now generally accepted that the better of the two for landscape planting – distinguished by its twigs more or less covered with tiny grey warts and leaves similarly rough to the touch – should be called *Betula pendula* (*B. verrucosa*). Pure stands of shapely trees can be seen around Inverness. The other type, *B. pubescens*, the Downy or White Birch, is frequently found on ill-drained acid soils. Its twigs and leaves are downy. Except for planting in such difficult positions it has no particular merit in our landscape. Being quick-growing the Silver Birch is valuable for early effect, either on its own or used as a nurse-tree for slower-growing species. The striking appearance of the white trunks is most noticeable in early spring when the twigs take on a purplish hue. The male catkins are very effective just before the leaves open, and the tiny foliage is never so conspicuous as when it turns yellow in autumn, presenting, particularly after rain, a glittering assembly, as of gold-dust. In a plantation the trees retain their somewhat conical crowns and do not blend into a uniform canopy; pruning or lopping of any kind, apart from the removal of stem-shoots, results in disaster.

To the forester a birch is a weed, like Sycamore and alder, and I suppose the Horse Chestnut. When working with those of a forester's outlook I have sometimes found it quite difficult to argue conclusively for the retention of even a few birches in a plantation, either scattered or *en masse*. But perseverance works wonders and birches continue to be left and even planted! Both species thrive on any normal soil but are less reliable on chalk and clay.

B. pendula 'Tristis' is a tall weeping form to be chosen in preference to the small, popular *B.p.* 'Youngii' where this kind of tree is needed in the foreground.

Dramatic contrast of lush valley growth with the bald hilltop of Tal-y-fan, North Wales. The two birches increase the sense of perspective without obscuring the view. The copse of oak shuts out the second meadow; the gap could be widened with advantage.

Buxus Box

Species	D/E	Approx. Height	Native Habitat	Date of Introduction
B. sempervirens Common Box	E	3–4·5 m 10–15 ft	Europe (Britain), N. Africa, W. Asia	

The Common Box is a small-leafed shrub achieving 12–15 ft or more in old age, on suitable ground. It is comparatively slow-growing, but one of its assets is that it will thrive on chalk – though it will grow equally well on any well-drained soil. It also flourishes in shade, and is therefore a useful shrub to replace the ubiquitous laurel and Pontic Rhododendron, thriving where yew is the only other permissible evergreen. The flowers are inconspicuous, mere yellowish tassels, but give off a sweet fragrance; in fact the fragrance of the bush, to some delightful, to others objectionable, lasts throughout the year. It is probably a native of Britain, and gives its name to Box Hill, Surrey, where very large old specimens abound.

CARPINUS   Hornbeam

Species	D/E	Approx. Height	Native Habitat	Date of Introduction
C. betulus Common Hornbeam	D	15–21 m 50–70 ft	Europe (S.E. England), Asia Minor	

The Hornbeam reaches a considerable size in nature but is seldom a dominant tree, nor is it a tree of heavy calibre. Perhaps it is most valuable as an understorey in woodland, where its ferny grace is specially appreciated. A long-lived tree, it thrives on any good soil, even sand and heavy clay. The small beech-like leaves are prettily tinted when young, mid-green all summer and yellow in the autumn. The small yellowish catkins are conspicuous at the moment when the tiny leaves develop. The grey, twisted, convoluted trunks are of great beauty. In the distance fully grown trees create a dense, dull canopy of small leaves: it is thus a tree which tends to disappear into the background rather than stand out. The form known as 'Fastigiata' (*C.b. pyramidalis*) makes a compact wide cone or almost a globe and is unsuitable for landscape planting.

CASTANEA   Chestnut

Species	D/E	Approx. Height	Native Habitat	Date of Introduction
C. sativa (C. vesca) Sweet or Spanish Chestnut	D	25–30 m 80–100 ft	S. Europe, N. Africa, Asia Minor	

There are few more majestic trees than an old Spanish or Sweet Chestnut. Its flowers, long creamy wisps held in bunches, do not appear until midsummer when most other trees are out of flower. The large glossy foliage gives a rich dark effect in the distance, but reflects much light close at hand. The autumn colour is often brilliant, turning to bright brown and yellow. It is a tree which thrives on acid sandy soils where the drainage is good. Though not a native, it has for so long been grown in our parks and woodlands that it is perfectly admissible for planting. It was probably introduced to Britain by the Romans for the value of its chestnuts; after good warm summers these are produced in abundance.

It thrives best in our warmer counties. When suited, the trees are not only long-lived but capable of rejuvenation to a remarkable degree, both from natural die-back or damage and from pruning and reduction of dead branches. Thus an old and apparently decrepit tree may well live for another hundred years with a little attention. These old specimens are as valuable as oaks in parkland and are found in their glory in Petworth Park, West Sussex, and also at Polesden Lacey, Surrey; here they thrive on a thin, lime-free topsoil over chalk.

CEDRUS Cedar

Species	D/E	Approx. Height	Native Habitat	Date of Introduction
C. libani Lebanon Cedar	E	25–33 m 80–110 ft	Turkey and neighbouring districts	c. 1670
C. atlantica Atlas Cedar	E	25–33 m 80–110 ft	Algeria and Morocco	1840
C. deodara Deodar Cedar	E	28–33 m 90–110 ft	Himalaya from E. Afghanistan to Garwhal	1831

At Wilton House, Wiltshire, cedars are planted to commemorate successive important dates. The planting of a landscape should be a continuing effort, to avoid the problem of the bulk of the trees reaching old age together.

The Cedar of Lebanon introduced in the mid-seventeenth century has become accepted as part and parcel of the grounds of great houses and parks, despite its outline which is quite foreign to our native trees. There is no doubt that it is one of the noblest of all trees. It stands out among the conifers for its massive trunk and its more or less horizontal branches in maturity. It is the extreme in horizontal line, just as the Wellingtonia and the Lombardy Poplar are in vertical line. Seldom do any of these striking trees need planting in bulk; one or a few are usually enough to hold the eye in any landscape. The characteristic growth of mature Lebanon Cedars is of no less value than their rich dark greenery.

The Atlas Mountains Cedar usually has greyish green needles and a more erect habit, with branches ascending at a more acute angle. The most commonly planted type is the Blue Cedar; the majority of these are vegetatively propagated and make remarkably uniform trees. The acute branching angle makes these trees more vulnerable to storm damage than the Lebanon Cedar, which also tends to live longer.

The splendidly graceful and luxuriant Deodar Cedar fits less easily into the landscape and is more suitable to large lawns. Its spire-like habit and drooping branchlets easily distinguish it. This is a quick-growing tree; the other two are by no means slow but the Lebanon in particular expends a lot of energy in growing side shoots and subsidiary leaders. All three grow best in the warmer counties of Britain and seed-raised trees vary considerably; they thrive on good deep soil and even in dry conditions on sand.

I think it must be admitted that Cedars are best placed within a short distance of the dwelling (witness the great tree at Farnborough Hall); they are less appropriate in the landscape. The mature old specimen at Scotney Castle, Kent, takes charge of the idyllic view subtly and ably.

CHAMAECYPARIS   Cypress
(see also CUPRESSUS)

Species	D/E	Approx. Height	Native Habitat	Date of Introduction
C. lawsoniana Lawson's Cypress	E	25–30 m 80–100 ft	Western N. America	1854

This species exhibits perhaps the greatest variation in cultivation of any imported tree, but here we are not concerned with the garden forms. It can only be considered a worthy tree for our landscape for one reason: the speed with which, as a variable seed-raised tree, it will achieve a non-uniform screen – though it should be used strictly temporarily while hollies and yews, for instance, are growing up. The variably tapering columns of dark bluish greenery are foreign to our landscape. The tree will thrive on a variety of soils except chalk and clay – though even on these it is sometimes successful. In the mass this species makes a gloomy company.

CORNUS   Dogwood

Species	D/E	Approx. Height	Native Habitat	Date of Introduction
C. sanguinea Common Dogwood	D	2–3 m 6–10 ft	Europe (S. England)	
C. alba Siberian Dogwood	D	2–3 m 6–10 ft	Siberia, China	1841

The native Common Dogwood is a dense bush of dark warm colouring in both autumn and winter; reddish plum-colour is a good description for the autumn colour of the leaves and of the winter twigs. It is particularly useful on chalk – as may be seen on the back slopes of Box Hill – but will grow on almost any reasonably drained soil. The leaves are dark green in summer, and tiny white flowers are produced, followed by black berries.

The Siberian Dogwood is a coarse-growing shrub, whose branches not only sucker from the root, but root wherever they touch the ground, making a vast thicket. It is a splendid ground-covering bush for most normal fertile soils and particularly on marshy ground. Copious mid-green leaves give good autumn colour together with clusters of blue-white berries which follow heads of tiny white flowers. It blends well with the native vegetation, but its chief merit is the plum-crimson tint of the winter twigs. Few sights are more warming than a belt of this shrub by the waterside, backed by some of the orange-red willows, when lit by the sun. Though the native dogwood varies somewhat from plant to plant, the Siberian seems to vary only in its lighter form 'Sibirica', the Westonbirt Dogwood. This is however a choicer plant, more suited to the garden and arboretum. Unfortunately it is enjoyed by rabbits, whereas they do not touch *C. alba*.

CORYLUS   Hazel or Cobnut

Species	D/E	Approx. Height	Native Habitat	Date of Introduction
C. avellana Hazel or Cobnut	D	3–6 m 10–20 ft	Europe (Britain), W. Asia, N. Africa	
C. maxima Filbert	D	3–6 m 10–20 ft	S. Europe	1759

The catkins of the Hazel herald the spring directly the leaves have fallen. It is a valuable understorey shrub or shrubby tree, thriving in sun or shade and in limy or acid soils, light or heavy in texture, also on chalk itself. Apart from its yellow autumn colour it has little to recommend it scenically, being of a dull dark green all the summer. But its tolerance of shade and soils makes it invaluable for thickening open woodland along with holly, as a low-range screen, and as a source of nuts, pea sticks and good stakes. The Filbert is almost identical, but its nuts are longer and the husks protrude beyond the nuts. It has similar uses.

CRATAEGUS Hawthorn

Species	D/E	Approx. Height	Native Habitat	Date of Introduction
C. monogyna Common Hawthorn	D	6–9 m 20–30 ft	Europe (Britain) to Afghanistan	
C. oxyacantha Hawthorn or May	D	4·5–6 m 15–20 ft	Europe (Britain)	

In Britain this well-known hedging plant is represented by two species, *C. monogyna* and *C. oxyacantha*, the former being by far the more common. The latter is restricted to heavier soils and thin woodland in the south of the country. Either will make a small tree, the former being successful even on windswept hills; both species thrive on limy or acid soils but preferably limy, growing to perfection on our chalk and limestone uplands. The early leafing, the sheet of white blossom, and the abundant dark red autumn fruits have all endeared the tree to us. A group or plantation will make their own uniform canopy, and their spines give the reason for the word "spinney".

CUPRESSUS Cypress
(see also CHAMAECYPARIS)

Species	D/E	Approx. Height	Native Habitat	Date of Introduction
C. macrocarpa Monterey Cypress	E	18–28 m 60–90 ft	California	1838

This was at one time a popular hedging plant but when clipped it is prone to insect attack and is not resistant to our coldest winters. As a tree it cannot be called homogeneous with our natives, but it has its uses in the landscape,

In a landscape of small features, such as drumlins and spoil-heaps from ancient quarries, small trees are appropriate. Here Hawthorns link with the distant oak.

for it is one of the few tall evergreens that will grow and thrive in maritime districts. In old age in the south-west of Britain it assumes a windswept, often flat-topped appearance and may easily be mistaken for a Lebanon or Atlas Cedar. After having driven under what I thought was a Lebanon Cedar immediately prior to entering the drive at Trengwainton, Cornwall, for some years, I was amazed on a later visit to realise that it was in fact a Monterey Cypress.

Cupressus macrocarpa is variable in growth, being normally raised from seeds, though its yellow forms are vegetatively propagated; the first raised, *C.m.* 'Lutea', is hardier than the type, but of narrower outline and unsuitable for our purpose. The Monterey Cypress has the added advantages of being quick-growing and thriving on any well-drained soil including chalk. It is a useful tree for temporary windbreaks.

The Leyland Cypress (× *Cupressocyparis leylandii*) is a hybrid between *Cupressus macrocarpa* and *Chamaecyparis nootkatensis*. It is a popular hedging and screening tree, and may achieve a height of 30 m (100 ft). Its formal outline precludes its use in the landscape except as a temporary screen.

EUCALYPTUS Gum

Species	D/E	Approx. Height	Native Habitat	Date of Introduction
E. gunnii Cider Gum	E	18–30 m 60–100 ft	Tasmania	c. 1840

In a book devoted mainly to native trees it may come as a surprise to find this genus. Cider Gums in quantity would strike a distinctly outlandish note, but having seen a number of fine individual specimens, including those at Sheffield Park, East Sussex, I unhesitatingly recommend it for certain purposes. Although it comes from the Southern Hemisphere there is no more reason to reject it than to deny ourselves the pleasures of other"foreign" trees such as the Lebanon Cedar or the Holm Oak. I believe its advantages outweigh purist prejudices.

In the first place it is a quick-growing evergreen. Secondly its flowers are creamy-white, comparatively inconspicuous. Thirdly, in maturity, it develops into a large rounded crown, assorting well in shape with our natives. Its leaves are small, leaden green. It thrives on well-drained sandy and loamy soils, limy or acid, but may not be a success on chalk.

Like many quick-growing trees, the roots are not hesitant, and therefore

The evergreen but tender Eucalyptus globulus *at Mount Stewart (National Trust), County Down, Northern Ireland. A fast-growing tree for very mild climates only.*

The evergreen Eucalyptus gunnii *at Sheffield Park (a property of the National Trust), East Sussex, about 30 m (100 ft) high. It is suitable only for the warmest counties of Britain.*

the plants should be put in when only a few inches high (one year old); they will put on 1–2 m (3–6 ft) in their second and subsequent years. Planted at this size they should not require staking. In its native country the Cider Gum thrives in marshy conditions, but in Britain such damp ground is not necessary. Many trees have been planted throughout southern England of recent years,· and most have come through severe winters without harm; some, planted in small gardens in built-up areas, will cause trouble to the owners and neighbours in years to come. To obtain the hardiest strains it is essential to ascertain the provenance of seed; seeds should be acquired from upland stands in Tasmania, or from trees in this country. Even with this proviso, the Cider Gum may only prove resistant to extra severe winters – such as was experienced in western England in 1981–2 – in our warmest counties.

When some disaster occurs in a landscape and we long for a fast-growing evergreen, this may be the answer; it can certainly be recommended in such emergencies. Other tall quick-growing species such as *E. globulus* can be used in very mild climates, as at Mount Stewart, Co. Down, but they do not, on account of the colour and size of the leaves, merge so well into the English landscape. Being seed-raised, plants of both species exhibit considerable difference in growth and habit.

FAGUS   Beech

Species	D/E	Approx. Height	Native Habitat	Date of Introduction
F. sylvatica Common Beech	D	25–30 m 80–100 ft	Europe (S. England)	

The Common Beech is one of our most popular trees for landscape planting and was much favoured in the eighteenth century. It thrives on chalky or acid soils so long as they are well drained, and is a fairly quick grower. The canopy of an old plantation knits well into a continuous line, though composed of markedly ascending twigs. It is so dense in growth, and its roots are so near the surface, that it excludes almost all other growth beneath it. The fringe of a beech wood in winter is of special beauty with its grey trunks, surface roots and carpet of brown leaves and for this reason should be kept open to view. The young foliage is some of the most brilliant in May; the summer tint dark; the autumn a glory of bright brown, after which the fallen leaves give great contrast to the grey of the trunks. It is a quick grower when suited, particularly if nursed with birch or larch when young.

The Copper or Purple-leaf Beech, of which the best form is always a grafted tree, 'Rivers' Purple' or 'Riversii', is an upsetting sight in our green landscape, and can set at nought the most carefully conceived schemes when seen at a distance. It should occasionally be planted within the ambit of a dwelling, but not too near. The Cut-leaf or Fern-leaf Beech, *F.s.* 'Heterophylla' or 'Asplenifolia', makes a fine compact specimen tree, standing singly, but has no value in the landscape. The Dawyck Beech, *F.s.* 'Dawyck' or 'Fastigiata', is a slender, gently fastigiate tree curving upwards like smoke from a bonfire and can be used instead of the Lombardy Poplar on chalk.

The Weeping Beech, *F.s. pendula*, can be seen in more than one form in Britain and their origins are obscure. At Florence Court, Co. Fermanagh, may be seen immense round-topped specimens. It is the largest-growing of all hardy weeping trees, achieving its size long after a weeping willow will have grown up and decayed, but except for special positions it cannot be

Nature's unaided work with beech trees near Chanctonbury Ring, West Sussex.

recommended for the general landscape. It is better planted, like the Copper Beech, somewhere near the dwelling, and makes a wonderful lawn specimen.

No beeches respond to lopping of any kind.

FRAXINUS Ash

Species	D/E	Approx. Height	Native Habitat	Date of Introduction
F. excelsior Common Ash	D	25–38 m 80–120 ft	Europe (Britain), Caucasus	
F. americana White Ash	D	25–38 m 80–120 ft	Eastern N. America	1724

The Common Ash is a conspicuous tree in our landscapes, contributing many different and valuable characteristics. It is essentially an open tree,

A great ash tree dominates thorn trees, dewpond and, indeed, the whole landscape, at Inkpen Beacon, Berkshire.

usually thin enough to see through at least partially in the summer, while in winter its thick twigs and picturesque branching make it *the* foreground tree for artists of all kinds. Its shoots remain dormant until early summer, giving contrast with other trees already fledged, and the leaves drop in autumn usually while still green. The bunches of dark flowers are of little account in the landscape, but the massed twigs, pale greyish in tint, impart a remarkable effect in woodlands when the canopy is lit by the winter sun. It thrives in cool moist conditions particularly on limy soils and is remarkably quick-growing, but not of much use for screening.

The White Ash is a splendid tree of similar qualities and has the added advantage of growing well in dry positions. The Weeping Ash, a form of *F. excelsior*, has a firm vigorous outline in winter and in summer. The stem should be trained up to at least 3 m (10 ft). It is suitable for a position where the garden merges into the park, or to provide a weeping line in an area where the weeping willow would be too large.

ILEX   Holly

Species	D/E	Approx. Height	Native Habitat	Date of Introduction
I. aquifolium Common Holly	E	9–18 m 30–60 ft	Europe (Britain), W. Asia	
I. × *altaclarensis* 'Hodginsii'	E	9–15 m 30–50 ft	Hybrid	c. 1836

The Common Holly is an invaluable shrub for sandy and well-drained soils, acid or limy, but hungry chalk is not recommended. The glittering leaves enliven the landscape, and the woods in winter; the berries on females are well known. It is very tolerant of shade and,, unless its growth below is inhibited by too much cover, will remain clothed to the ground even in old age. It is raised from seed, so the desired gentle variation in growth is assured. As a woodland or spinney plant to provide low screening and shelter it is unequalled, but it is best transplanted when quite small and even then can be tricky unless prepared, nursery-grown stock is used, preferably in containers. When established its leaders will grow as much as 60 cm (2 ft) per year, but to bolster the screen during its early years some temporary evergreen can be employed, such as the Western Hemlock or × *Cupresso-cyparis leylandii*.

Beautiful though many of its selected clones may be, they have no place in the landscape; vegetatively propagated "free-berrying" clones should be avoided. An exception may be made for *I. × altaclerensis* 'Hodginsii' which is a particularly dense, hardy male clone with broad dark leaves. As a massive screen, invariably well clothed to the ground as long as its growth is uninhibited, it has no equal, but its uniformity is against it. It is good value by the sea and in industrial areas.

Conifers dominate the landscape at Tarn Hows, a National Trust property in Cumbria, sympathetically to the lie of the land. The gate and the winding roadway are attractive, but to complete a picture the wire fence needs obscuring and more junipers on the right would accentuate the curve of the road. Compare with the colour picture, plate 9.

JUNIPERUS Juniper

Species	D/E	Approx. Height	Native Habitat	Date of Introduction
J. communis Common Juniper	E	2–6 m 6–20 ft	N. Europe (Britain), S.W. Asia, N. America	

A shrub of wide distribution on limy and acid soils, but of little use in the landscape, except perhaps to colonise a barren chalky slope in southern Britain, or in like conditions elsewhere. Its tiny dark grey-green leaves provide a dense yew-like mass but its growth is not self-reliant, and is wayward in the extreme. It is very variable in habit.

LARIX Larch

Species	D/E	Approx. Height	Native Habitat	Date of Introduction
L. decidua (*L. europaea*) Common or European Larch	D	28–35 m 90–120 ft	Central Europe	early 17th cent.
L. kaempferi (*L. leptolepis*) Japanese Larch	D	25–30 m 80–100 ft	Japan	1861
L. × *eurolepis* Dunkeld or Hybrid Larch	D	25–30 m 80–100 ft	Hybrid	c. 1895

We are so accustomed to seeing and thinking of these trees as candidates for forestry that their appearance as mature isolated specimens is apt to be forgotten. They are of irregular open conical growth, beautiful in spring with bright green young foliage and again in late autumn when turning yellow. They are a good green in summer. The European Larch shows up well in the winter sunlight, having yellowish grey twigs, while the Japanese species is a reddish orange-brown. The foliage of the latter is a greyish green. The hybrid between the two is variable in tint of bark and foliage. First generation crosses are the best, producing vigorous, disease-resistant trees. The young foliage of all three sheds its fragrance in the air, and all bear small cones which hang on the twigs for a year or more. They are all useful for quick screening and for hastening slower trees by interplanting and their incidence in irregular groups in the largest landscapes is pleasing. They are best planted when quite small, and thrive on moist or dry open soils, but not on chalk or clay.

Ligustrum Privet

Species	D/E	Approx. Height	Native Habitat	Date of Introduction
L. vulgare Common Privet	Semi E	2–2·5 m 6–8 ft	Europe (Britain)	
L. ovalifolium Oval-leaf Privet	Semi E	2·5–3·8 m 8–12 ft	Japan	c. 1885

It frequently happens that an evergreen understorey is needed in thin woodland or along the fringes of spinneys. Our natives – holly, yew and box – are valuable for the purpose but there are two nearly evergreen shrubs in this genus which should not be forgotten. Like yew, our native, semi-evergreen Common Privet is invaluable in exposed places, even on hungry chalky soil, and its glistening black berries in autumn are of rare beauty. When in flower in July it provides a heady scent, like the Japanese species which is so popular as a hedging plant, but this latter grows best on sandy and good loamy soils, acid or limy. As a rule a limy soil results in *L. ovalifolium* remaining evergreen through all but the severest winter. This shrub is more successful than almost any other in disguising the fact that it is not a native. It will achieve some 3 m (10 ft), making wide, rounded, cumulous greenery of inestimable value on account of its light tint, a change from dark holly and gloomy yew. It thrives best in full sun, or in partly shaded positions. As a young plant, pruned, clipped or free-grown, it gives no indication of its gentle outline in maturity.

Malus Apple

Species	D/E	Approx. Height	Native Habitat	Date of Introduction
M. sylvestris Wild Crab	D	3–9 m 10–30 ft	Europe (Britain)	

One of the lesser trees, useful for the fringes of clumps and spinneys in the near distance, it has similar uses to the Rowan and Hawthorn. All of them give a touch of domesticity as opposed to the greater trees. The Crab Apple varies considerably but usually makes a low tree with a dense rounded head, covered with fragrant flowers from blush to deep pink in bud in late spring, and in good seasons hung with reddish small fruits in late summer and autumn. It is not particular about soil as long as it is not boggy. A more vigorous tree is the Siberian Crab (*M. baccata*) whose fruits, the size of a cherry, develop in autumn and hang on until late winter. The flowers are white. There are many hybrids, the best known being *M. × robusta*. This is propagated vegetatively but seed-raised stock is preferable for landscape planting.

MORUS   Mulberry

Species	D/E	Approx. Height	Native Habitat	Date of Introduction
M. alba White Mulberry	D	6–9 m 20–30 ft	China	c. 1596

A foreigner which I have included, in common with *Acer negundo*, because of its small height and light green foliage. It has been cultivated in Europe for centuries. It succeeds in the southern counties of Britain and should be planted in sunny positions.

NOTHOFAGUS   Southern Beech

Species	D/E	Approx. Height	Native Habitat	Date of Introduction
N. obliqua Roble	D	25–30 m 80–100 ft	S. America	1849
N. procera Rauli	D	25–30 m 80–100 ft	S. America	1910

The Southern Beeches are much to the fore these days among planters of woodland gardens. The above two species merge well with our native trees. They thrive in our warmer counties in open soil, acid or neutral, and are fast-growing, particularly *N. obliqua*. They have little beauty of flower, but their early leafing is an asset and their brilliant autumn colour – mostly yellow – a benison. They are not good wind-resisters and are thus best for valley planting and the infilling of woodlands.

The Roble seeds itself abundantly when suited, and is one of the quickest-growing trees for the British climate, but its outline is weak and unsatisfactory. The Rauli is more characterful in growth and foliage but is not quite so fast-growing. It is hardy only in the warmer counties. Both these species – and several others – are really more suited to gardens and arboreta than to our landscapes, though at a distance these two would be taken for natives.

PICEA   Spruce Fir

Species	D/E	Approx. Height	Native Habitat	Date of Introduction
P. abies (*P. excelsa*) Norwegian Spruce	E	28–30 m 90–100 ft	N. and S.E. Europe	17th cent.

In the eighteenth century the Norwegian or Common Spruce was frequently planted. Like the Scots Pine, its dark greenery gives an impression of shadow from clouds passing over a woodland. The Spruce is still a common conifer in our woods, though overtaken by the Sitka Spruce, *Picea sitchensis*, in forestry. Either will quickly make a screen, but neither can compete with the pines for picturesqueness; moreover the Sitka Spruce even in old age usually retains a spire-like top, breaking the line of the woods, whereas the Norwegian Spruce flattens out at the top and thus blends well with our native trees. It prefers a moist soil. Old books frequently refer to "firs", by which is usually meant Scots Pine.

PINUS   Pine

Species	D/E	Approx. Height	Native Habitat	Date of Introduction
P. sylvestris Scots Pine	E	21–28 m 70–90 ft	N. Old World (Britain)	
P. nigra Austrian Pine	E	21–28 m 70–90 ft	S.E. Europe	1835
P. pinaster (*P. maritima*) Maritime Pine	E	28–30 m 90–100 ft	S.W. Europe, N. Africa	16th cent.
P. radiata (*P. insignis*) Monterey Pine	E	25–30 m 80–100 ft	California	1833

Of all the conifers, these four pines seem to blend best into our landscapes. This is partly because when mature they tend to lose the pointed top of most other conifers, they do not exceed the height of our native trees, and of course we already have a native pine. The Scots Pine is, I think, the most beautiful of all pines, with its mature bark of pinkish brown in marked contrast to the soft grey-green colour of its needles, and its picturesque shape in maturity. No two trees are ever the same. In England the Scots Pine is generally slim with a rounded head; we have to go to the ancient Caledonian forests to see it in its grandest form. There is no doubt that it is

The Scots Pine is a good tree to have near at hand on account of the beautiful soft pinkish-brown colour of its bark. Taken in North Wales, this photograph shows the importance of human habitation – in the vernacular – in the landscape. To make a successful picture an artist would have included some shrubs in the left foreground.

our foremost landscape conifer, and it thrives best in deep sandy or loamy soils, preferably acid, and where the drainage is good. On chalk soils and heavy clays we have an excellent substitute in the Austrian Pine, which in maturity usually assumes similarly picturesque shapes. Like the Scots Pine it frequently has two or three stems when well spaced. Its foliage is a particularly dark green and its stems are dark grey-brown – both entitling it to the epithet "gloomy" – and it is the right choice on almost any soil in windy positions where its rugged appearance lends enchantment to grey stone castles and ruins. It was chosen for planting one side of the first glimpse towards the great grey castle at Penrhyn, Gwynedd, for the sake of its rugged darkness which will, we hope, be prominent in a hundred years. Its close relative the Corsican Pine (*Pinus nigra maritima* or *P.n. laricio*) is by contrast a stiff, tall, soldierly tree of quick growth rarely suitable for anything but forestry.

The Maritime Pine has a colourful bark similar to that of the Scots Pine and in maturity, as at Sheffield Park, it makes a picturesque rounded head above a tall stem. It is coarse-needled and very quick-growing on deep good soil or almost pure sands; it withstands sea winds well.

In maritime districts and elsewhere in the southern and western counties of these islands the Monterey Pine stands pre-eminent on account of its rich greenery and rapid growth, while as an old tree it develops a large rounded head, becoming gaunt and wide-branched, every branch adding to its touch of age by retaining many years of cone-production. Like the Maritime Pine it is resistant to sea-winds, and thrives in any well-drained soil, particularly on sand. The many other beautiful foreign pines are more suited to the lawn than the landscape.

Pines should all be planted when quite young. It is better to use one-year seedlings of the Monterey Pine than pot-grown youngsters.

Austrian Pines give a similarly Picturesque outline to Scots Pines in maturity, and are more successful in extreme exposure on poor chalky or clay soils. The nature reserve on Island Reagh, Strangford Lough, Northern Ireland, protected by the National Trust.

In suitably moist meadowland the London Plane is the largest and most majestic of trees that can be grown in southern England. This extra large tree, with two trunks, is at Mottisfont Abbey, Hampshire (National Trust).

PLATANUS   Plane

Species	D/E	Approx. Height	Native Habitat	Date of Introduction
P. orientalis Oriental Plane	D	25–30 m 80–100 ft	S.E. Europe	16th cent.
P. acerifolia London Plane	D	28–35 m 90–120 ft	Hybrid	mid–18th cent.

The Oriental Plane is looked upon with special delight by planters of trees. It is usually as wide as it is high and its deeply cut leaves give it a more delicate appearance than the coarse large leaves of its hybrids. It blends well with British natives, and though not noteworthy for its spring or autumn tints has a special value in the landscape for its light green tint throughout the summer. The winter display of its fruits – "bobbles" – is noticeable.

Its hybrid the London Plane is at once the tallest and most graceful of large-growing trees for our warmer counties, where conditions are also favourable to the Oriental Plane. They both thrive particularly in moist meadowland, limy or otherwise, though the London Plane will survive and even grow well in poor and restricted town sites. They are not happy in windy uplands. The large size of the London Plane's leaves makes it a conspicuous tree; it is useful for accentuating perspectives, but can easily be overdone in the landscape. Moreover, both the Oriental and London Planes are propagated vegetatively and, in spite of some variants within Britain, present a uniformity which is not suitable for informal planting.

To see plane trees in their full majesty one should go to Mottisfont, Hampshire, where the London Plane has produced a specimen – with two trunks and an outlying, self-layered extra – which can only be described as marvellous. It is possibly the largest tree of any kind in these islands.

POPULUS   Poplar

Species	D/E	Approx. Height	Native Habitat	Date of Introduction
P. nigra Black Poplar	D	28–30 m 90–100 ft	W. Eurasia	
P.n. betulifolia Downy Black Poplar or Manchester Poplar	D	21–28 m 70–90 ft	W. Europe (Britain)	
P.n. italica Lombardy Poplar	D	28–30 m 90–100 ft	N. Italy	18th cent.
P. simonii 'Fastigiata'	D	18 m 60 ft	N. and W. China	1913
P. × canadensis 'Serotina' Black Italian Poplar	D	28–38 m 90–130 ft	Hybrid	early 18th cent.
P. × canadensis 'Robusta' Robusta Poplar	D	28–38 m 90–130 ft	Hybrid	1895
P. canescens Grey Poplar	D	28–30 m 90–100 ft	Hybrid	

Species	D/E	Approx. Height	Native Habitat	Date of Introduction
P. alba White Poplar, Abele	D	15–18 m 50–60 ft	Eurasia, N. Africa	
P. tremula Aspen	D	9–12 m 30–40 ft	N. Old World (Britain), Algeria	
P. trichocarpa Black Cottonwood	D	30–47 m 100–150 ft	Western N. America	end 19th cent.

Taken collectively the poplars present a greater variation of tints through the year than any other group of trees except the willows. Together they form a diversified collection of trees and large shrubs which are valued for their rapidity of growth and tolerance of moist or wet soils. While the willows excel in growth from 3 m to 21 m (10 ft to 70 ft) or so, the poplars stand higher, from 12 m to 38 m (40 ft to 130 ft). They can be used together with great advantage, giving a totally different impression from our usual native hardwoods. They at once bring a lithe, light touch to the landscape and though some are not tall they give an overall feeling of reaching upwards, like a gothic building.

Whenever poplars are mentioned the uninitiated tend to think solely of the Lombardy Poplar. Over the years I have learnt that this is not only due to ignorance of what other poplars there may be, but also to a prejudice about coarse growth, greedy roots and other problems. No doubt much of the prejudice is justified but anyone who has seen a big specimen of our native Black Poplar cannot but grant it pride of place among poplars, and admit that it can compare favourably with any other of our greater trees. It was called the Herculean Poplar by the ancients. Most poplars lean away from the prevailing wind and the Black Poplar is no exception. It may be called black because of the great burrs or bosses on the rugged trunk which are of black appearance; they are repeated on the largest, lowest branches which always arch downwards, nearly to the ground. Added to their magnificent port and their yellow autumn colour is the spectacle of their March display of catkins, which are conspicuously crimson on male trees until the pollen is released. The Black Poplar grows across England from East Anglia to Herefordshire in the main, nearly always by ditches and streams or in the hedgerows of moist meadows.

The botanical status of the native type is *P.n. betulifolia*, the Downy Black or Manchester Poplar. One seldom sees a middle-aged tree and as a consequence it is difficult to reconcile young trees of some 12 m (40 ft), with their

A landscape on a large scale at Lake Hayes, South Island, New Zealand. This superb view of hills and water is dramatically contrasted by the strong groups of Lombardy Poplars and softened by the silvery rounded tops of willows.

Dunster Castle, a property of the National Trust. The mixture of tints from the foliage of different trees is enlivened by the vertical line of the Lombardy Poplars. As a picture, the view is spoiled by the row of trees following the line of a fence in the mid-foreground.

dense twiggy growth, to the gaunt arching specimens a hundred years old or more. This species was, apart from the White, the Grey and the little Aspen, the only free-growing poplar known in Britain before the introduction of the North American species and their hybrids. These hybrids today far outnumber all other poplars put together throughout the country. But nurseries have for long distributed with confidence the *P.n. betulifolia* under the descriptive and qualifying name of Manchester Poplar, as it thrives in poor conditions alike of soil and air. It creates a dense twiggy tree of great value in screening, even in winter, but is slow-growing.

The Lombardy Poplar has been grown in Britain since the end of the eighteenth century. A splendid dramatic tree, it has been adopted in our countryside with the same enthusiasm as those other trees of foreign importation and horizontal line, the cedars. Among large trees no greater contrast in shape can be found. The Lombardy is the ideal tree when an exclamation mark in the landscape is required. Unfortunately it is most often planted in a row, although isolated specimens or small irregular groups are more effective. Used in flat meadows and other reasonably moist ground they achieve a great majesty, and in such settings, where their tops do not project above the skyline of hill or tree clump, they are an asset to planting schemes. Trees described as Lombardy Poplars vary considerably in growth. Apart from the difference in vigour of trees in moist meadows or dry clay or chalky eminences (which do not suit any poplars), we may note that the original type is susceptible to a foliage disease and skinny, early-defoliated trees usually indicate that this trouble is present on the original male type of Lombardy. There are several other types available, the most magnificent, vigorous and disease-resistant being the cultivar 'Plantierensis', which can be male or female; another excellent large type is 'Gigantea', a female, which forms a wide column.

The Lombardy grows best in a loose normal soil; for a vertical line on pure chalk the Dawyck Beech should be used instead and on heavy clay it is best to consider the Fastigiate Oak. There is another worthy fastigiate poplar, *P. simonii* 'Fastusiata' (*P. simonii obtusata*), whose slender branches ascend in a snake-like way; one might think it had been the model for Van Gogh's fastigiate trees. It is much smaller, and slower in growth, than the Lombardy and is thus suitable for restricted areas. In height it may achieve 18 m (60 ft). Its leaves are shiny, dark green and obovate.

The next most common poplar in the southern half of England is the group headed by *P.* × *canadensis* (or *P.* × *euamericana*), hybrids between *P. nigra* and the North American *P. deltoides*, the Eastern Cottonwood. In the main these are timber trees but they have several assets for landscape planting: speed of growth on any reasonably retentive soil, great height, and the best clones are resistant to canker. These hybrids do not thrive so well farther north, which is another reason why the Manchester Poplar has held its own in competition with them. The best known is given the misleading and confusing name "Black Italian Poplar". It is a gigantic tree achieving greater height more quickly than any other (unless beaten by some of the newer poplars) and therefore of great value as a screen or as a height-giver in the distance. Its grey bark uniformly furrowed is a noticeable winter feature, and this applies to all the clones, likewise the mid-green leaves which turn to clear yellow in autumn. Its other characteristic, that of late leafing (as indicated by its Latin name), can be both an asset and a disadvantage. It is an asset because by remaining dormant into late spring it escapes possible frost damage and also prolongs that delightful period, common to both spring and autumn, when trees are not uniformly fledged. It becomes a disadvantage when the tree is used as a wind screen: the late leafing affords no protection against the cold winds of earliest spring. The young foliage of the whole group provides a warm coppery brownish tint after we have experienced the beauty of the crimson male catkins; all three varieties included here are male clones.

When in an isolated position, the Black Italian normally has a somewhat leaning trunk of some 9–12 m (30–40 ft), above which the head of branches is arranged like the fingers of the open hand, with the thumb towards the prevailing wind and curving in towards the widespread crown. Planted in a group of, say, six or eight trees it will provide a wide-topped, park-type clump of great size and height. In both instances it is a tree of great character, to be used sparingly in the landscape and valued for its rapid growth. When planted closely as a screen or for timber, it develops a narrow outline and is obviously a foreign tree. Its use in the landscape can only be excused when there is a need for height.

'Robusta' is a more symmetrical tree of narrower outline and has supplanted 'Serotina' as a timber tree in Britain on account of its erect stem and uniform growth. It is conspicuous in early spring because of its crimson catkins, shortly followed by its early-flushing coppery brown young foliage. This early flush makes it particularly valuable where protection to a garden is needed against spring winds. The genuine 'Eugenei' is another useful hybrid poplar of great vigour.

Another large tree is the magnificent Grey Poplar. On a big specimen the black "necklaces" of the lenticels are noticeable on the yellowish-grey bark, markedly distinct from any other tree. Though black and corky on the trunk, the yellowish grey of the bark is conspicuous far up into the crown and gives a remarkable contrast in March when male trees are freely hung with crimson catkins. In spring its leaves are grey, with a lustrous dark green upper surface; this rich green persists until the yellowing of autumn. The head is large and untidy with many ascending branches pointing away from the prevailing wind; the branches are heavily twigged and are apt to break and fall. The duration in unharmed majesty of this tree is therefore relatively short. It rejuvenates well both from the stem and from the ground as it suckers freely, but unlike the foregoing poplars and the Aspen it does not root readily from cuttings. A good tree in its prime has few rivals. It is presumed to be a hybrid between the White Poplar and the Aspen.

Of all poplars the White perhaps leans away from the wind more than any; in fact it is only in sheltered places that it retains a vertical habit. It is not an imposing tree, though capable of attaining a good height; its leaning, wayward growth and general light colouring make it suitable for foreground planting. The grey bark, speckled with black lenticels, gives way to black corky excrescences at the base. The foliage in spring is silvery white and the undersides of the lobed leaves remain silvery-grey until they fall in autumn, when the dark green upper surfaces turn to bright yellow; at this time they make a beautiful pattern on the ground. Most of the trees I have seen are female with small greenish catkins. It is a freely suckering tree, and, like the Grey Poplar, will do well on limy and drier land.

The widely fastigiate form from Central Asia, *P.a.* 'Pyramidalis', has not the distinct columnar line of the Lombardy Poplar and is best omitted from the landscape and left to collectors of the peculiar.

The Aspen, a freely suckering slender tree of little account in the landscape, is our smallest poplar, but also the noisiest. Its leaf-stalks are remarkably flattened and the blades flutter and clatter in every breeze. The catkins are large, like great grey hairy caterpillars, the male being the more conspicuous in size and colour. The leaves are dull green through the summer turning to butter yellow in autumn.

Most poplars give off a pungent aromatic odour, particularly in spring and when the leaves have fallen; on a warm autumn day on damp grass the fragrance is all-pervading. The most fragrant are the Balsam Poplars of North America, of which the Black Cottonwood is the species most frequently planted in Britain; a few trees to windward will provide a rich balsamic odour on the air. The odour is remarkably lasting; if the yellow exudation from the bud touches the tip of the nose it will remain potent until washed off. The Black Cottonwood is a tree of considerable vigour, with strong erect growth. Female trees bear small catkins but make up for this when fruiting, for they distribute masses of "cotton" which gives the trees their name of Cottonwood. The white cotton is poured forth in great abundance and can be a nuisance if the trees are near the garden. The reddish catkins on male trees are conspicuous but it is the leaves which make this type so noticeable. They are of normal poplar size on small branches, but those on the leading shoots are very large; this is coupled with the fact that at about 12 m (40 ft) the trees usually develop several leading shoots which give them a top-heavy appearance. These topmost branches are inclined to break. The clone or clones in cultivation are susceptible to canker, and when all is considered this is not a tree which fits well into the native landscape. Its merits lie in its gigantic growth when used as a temporary screen or filler, its fragrance, and in its early leafing. A new clone raised in North America, 'Fritzi Pauley', has proved canker-resistant so far and where a fast temporary tree is needed for lush meadow-planting this should be chosen.

Poplars are great producers of timber, and in evaluating the numerous hybrids and forms the forestry experts have been much influenced by the bulk of the trunk at a given age, which has somewhat clouded their assessment of them for landscape uses. Having recently seen many at the Forestry Commission's plantations at Alice Holt, Farnham, Surrey, under the guidance of Mr Alan Mitchell, I have unhesitatingly chosen the few mentioned at the expense of many newer timber-producing clones.

Pollinated by *P. trichocarpa*, *P. maximowiczii* has produced the hybrid 'Androscoggin', which is of extremely rapid growth. Like the Black Cottonwood it has, however, failings in regard to canker. At one time the commonest balsam poplar in Britain, the Ontario or Balm of Gilead Poplar is now seldom seen, being very susceptible to canker; I only hope that its revolting variegated form 'Aurora' will succumb soon to the same fate. Its only possible merit is found in its use as a hard-pruned bush in a garden where variegation is not only tolerated but enjoyed.

I think that, having devoted more space to poplars than to any other genus, I should reiterate that only the Black, the Grey, the White and the Aspen can be said to blend into our natural scene. The Lombardy is an exception to every rule but has its special value. The × *canadensis* hybrids and the Black Cottonwood are a very different matter. It is normal to reproduce poplars vegetatively. Uniformity is not so noticeable in wayward trees such as the Black and the Grey Poplar, and with the Lombardy it is an asset; the Aspen is seldom planted in quantity and when it is it grows irregularly. The danger of creating a foreign appearance arises with the × *canadensis* poplars and the Black Cottonwood. When well spaced, 'Robusta' and the Black Cottonwood make splendid trees, but uniform in outline. The massed plantings of 'Serotina' make some of the ugliest belts in the country; planted too closely they cannot achieve their real majesty, which is, however, still of an outlandish nature. In conclusion these poplars should always be *well spaced* and should only be used when no other tree of such great height and rapid growth is available.

PRUNUS   Cherry, Plum, Laurel

Species	D/E	Approx. Height	Native Habitat	Date of Introduction
P. avium Gean, Mazzard or Common Cherry	D	12–21 m 40–70 ft	Europe (Britain)	

Species	D/E	Approx. Height	Native Habitat	Date of Introduction
P. padus Bird Cherry	D	9–15 m 30–50 ft	Old World (Britain)	
P. serotina Rum or Black Cherry	D	12–25 m 40–80 ft	N. America	1629
P. cerasifera Cherry Plum, Myrobalan	D	6–9 m 20–30 ft	A cultivated tree	
P. spinosa Sloe, Blackthorn	D	2·5–3·8 m 8–12 ft	Europe (Britain), N. Asia	
P. laurocerasus Cherry Laurel	E	3–9 m 10–30 ft	S.E. Europe, S.W. Asia	end 16th cent.
P. lusitanica Portuguese Laurel	E	3–6 m 10–20 ft	Spain and Portugal	c. 1648

Without doubt the Gean or Mazzard is not only a genuine native but is also highly acceptable in the landscape, contributing a haze of white flowers in spring and brilliant autumn colour. It is one of the very few medium-sized trees, but sometimes achieves as much as 25 m (80 ft). Its quick growth is a valuable asset and it thrives on a variety of well-drained soils heavy or light, acid or limy, including chalk, throughout the country. It is raised from seeds and growth is varied; it sows itself and also reproduces from suckers. It is an ordinary mid-green in summer and as a group provides a uniform canopy in time. It is intolerant of shade. As a light touch to the landscape in spring and autumn it has much to recommend it.

The Bird Cherry is found as a native mainly in the north and west of Britain, particularly on limy soils. Its spikes of off-white flowers are strongly but scarcely pleasantly scented in early summer, and for this reason it is best kept away from the landscape areas around the house, and it does not excel in autumn colour, though its clear green foliage is noticeable in summer. It is a small tree, but larger than Hawthorn and Crab. A close relative, the Rum Cherry of eastern North America, is very similar though of larger growth, and seeds itself plentifully in light soils. The leaves are of shining green and turn yellow in autumn.

The Myrobalan Plum used to be a popular hedging plant and as a consequence in March some overgrown hedgerows are a sheet of white blossom. As the flowering usually coincides with cold winds, one frequently hears the Myrobalan being mistaken for Blackthorn which does not flower until a month later. Sometimes crops of red or yellow plums mature. It is a fast-growing thicket-maker with fresh green summer foliage and thrives on any soil, acid or limy.

The Blackthorn or Sloe frequents mainly limy soils and forms an impenetrable prickly thicket; it has small dark green leaves in summer, white flowers in April and blue-black sloes in October. It is a useful shrub for forming thickets on chalk in windswept areas, spreading mainly by suckers. All of the above species are usually raised from seeds.

The Common or Cherry Laurel, *Prunus laurocerasus*, was introduced into Britain in the late sixteenth century. Two hundred years later it was recognised as being perfectly hardy and was recommended by Sir Uvedale Price for underplanting in eighteenth-century landscape gardens. The results of this fashion can be seen at Stourhead, Wiltshire, and Claremont, Surrey. Its rich array of shining bright green leaves must have been a welcome sight among our few dark evergreen natives. If grown from seed it will in sheltered conditions preserve its leader and make a wide, graceful small tree. Several types are available from nurserymen in quantity, all propagated vegetatively: 'Rotundifolia' is a somewhat yellowish green, to be avoided; 'Caucasica' is a compact grower with rather erect narrow leaves, also to be avoided; with large droopy leaves and vigorous growth is 'Magnoliifolia' (also known as 'Latifolia'). This is a conspicuous shrub even in a garden devoted to large-leafed rhododendrons. But the Common Laurel, also usually grown from cuttings, is the best for underplanting and screening and if the plants have been raised from seeds so much the better. The spikes of white flowers in spring are followed in summer in favourable seasons by plentiful "cherries", nearly black, which germinate freely. Heeled cuttings may be rooted easily in the open ground in early autumn.

The broad leaves of these laurels reflect much light and thereby reduce the perspective. They all thrive on almost any soil but are inclined to become chlorotic and poor on chalk. In woodlands where they are growing well they may reach 7·5 m (25 ft) and are vigorous spreaders, rooting as they go.

Without doubt many rude words have been expressed against the Common Laurel because of its luxuriant, fast-spreading growth (see also *Rhododendron ponticum*). Through the centuries since its introduction it has been alternately praised or cursed according to how much labour has been available to keep it under control.

The Portuguese Laurel is considerably more tree-like than the Common or Cherry Laurel, and instead of forming a mass of semi-procumbent branches it makes a wide rounded head some 6 m (20 ft) or more high and wide. The smaller leaves are of a dull dark green, cheered up by reddish stalks; its flowers, borne in slender spikes, are creamy and do not appear until early summer, and are followed by red berries turning nearly to black. Its self-reliant habit promotes it into use alongside yew and holly, though it is not quite so tolerant of overhead shade. For low screening the Cherry

Laurel is better as the Portuguese tends to bare its stems with age. It is normally propagated by seeds and varies very little in habit; the seeds germinate freely and it seldom layers itself. The variant from the Azores, *P.l. azorica*, is equally hardy and a far more handsome tree, remaining dense and bushy to the ground. The leaves are rather more attractive but otherwise its separate value for landscape planting is not great.

PYRUS   Pear

Species	D/E	Approx. Height	Native Habitat	Date of Introduction
P. communis Common Pear	D	10·5–15 m 35–50 ft	Europe (Britain)	

The Common Pear is occasionally seen as a wild tree in Britain and is conspicuous in early spring when its copious white blossom precedes other kinds of "flowering" trees. Some of the forms and hybrids grown for the production of perry are equally tall and imposing. It is deep-rooted and thrives best on deep soils. The small, glossy, dark green leaves do not usually give autumn colour. The fruits are small, green and unpalatable. Since it is freely used as an understock for standard pears it is usually available seed-raised.

QUERCUS   Oak

Species	D/E	Approx. Height	Native Habitat	Date of Introduction
Q. robur (*Q. pedunculata*) Common, English or Pedunculate Oak	D	18–30 m 60–100 ft	Europe (Britain), Caucasus	
Q. petraea (*Q. sessiliflora*) Durmast or Sessile Oak	D	18–30 m 60–100 ft	Europe (Britain)	
Q. cerris Turkish Oak	D	30–38 m 100–120 ft	S. and Central Europe	c. 1735
Q. ilex Holm Oak, Ilex Oak	E	18–25 m 60–80 ft	Mediterranean Region	16th cent.

It is curious that our usual conception of an oak – a wide-thrusting, powerful-looking tree – should have been acquired mainly because it was so often planted singly in the past to produce "elbowed" branches for building ships. Grown in woods the oak achieves great height but as a

By the removal of a horizontal hedge, and the thinning of a row of trees, these two pictures, from Repton's Observations, 1805, *show an improvement in a landscape peopled with English Oak.*

singleton in clearances or hedgerows it is a totally different tree, of great majesty.

The most important point for us to grasp is the difference in terrain and district where our two natives occur. The English Oak frequents the lowlands especially in the southern half of England, where its bulky form is easily recognised – usually a large stout trunk supporting outward-thrusting branches of great diversity of line. Its leaves are short-stalked but the acorns are borne on long stalks or peduncles. In the Sessile or Durmast Oak the leaves and acorns have no stalks. The latter makes a free-growing, tall, upward-thrusting tree and is much more common on hilly ground, particularly in the north and west. When drawn up as a forest tree the Sessile Oak can be quite tall and even slender, though isolated specimens sometimes approach the majesty of the English Oak. Both have the same characteristic foliage effect, the Sessile often resisting the attacks of the *Tortrix* moth better. They are late in leafing in the spring; when birches, elms and beeches are of brilliant green the sallow or brownish tones of the oaks make a wonderful contrast until the leaves are fully unfolded. There is every possible variation of tint and timing in a plantation of oaks both in spring and again in autumn, when their leaves seem reluctant to take on their russet or yellowish tones. Though their canopy of leaves may be dense, some shrubs flourish beneath them, partly because the main feeding roots strike downwards.

An excellent vertical line for heavy clay soils where the Lombardy Poplar may not thrive is found in *Q. robur fastigiata*. There appear to be at least two clones of this in general use in this country; the narrowest should be chosen. There is an excellent example at Wisley. Two distinct clones are growing at Cliveden, Buckinghamshire, in two places in the garden, but particularly opposite the Blenheim Pavilion.

The Turkey or Turkish Oak is perfectly permissible for planting in our landscapes for the simple reason that it is very similar in general appearance to our natives, but is much quicker in growth. In these days of long neglect it is therefore valuable, notably because it will thrive on poor and chalky soils as well as on good loam. Its spring tints are unremarkable, but its leaves turn to a bright brown in autumn while during the summer it gives the darkest of greens apart from conifers. As a dark background to an Oriental Plane, for instance, no deciduous tree can give greater contrast. A large tree can compete with any other in majesty. Its timber is of little value, but this need not concern us here.

Our fourth oak is of very different appearance. It is the Holm or Ilex Oak, an evergreen with unique qualities which make it indispensable for certain planting schemes, and through long usage – it was introduced from the Mediterranean region in the sixteenth century – it has become as much part of our parklands as the Lebanon Cedar. It will thrive on chalky soils or on any well-drained medium (except in the north of Scotland) and is an excellent wind-resister even near the sea. Fortunately it makes a large rounded tree which, apart from being evergreen, blends happily in the English landscape. Unless eaten by animals it keeps its lower branches clothed almost to the ground and is therefore an ideal screen from 1 m (3 ft) upwards. Its sombre green is enlivened in early summer when the young foliage develops its silvery tint. Though not of course a disadvantage in parkland, its acorns and foliage are a menace to lawn mowers, and the leaves, falling as they do in early summer, are cursed by most gardeners.

During the disastrous icy spell of the winter of 1981/2, Holm Oaks suffered badly, particularly in the west of England. The leaves turned brown and many twigs and branches – even trees – were killed. I believe this is the first time that this tree has suffered in this country since its introduction in the sixteenth century, but it is a warning to rely upon it only in our warmest counties.

RHODODENDRON

Species	D/E	Approx. Height	Native Habitat	Date of Introduction
R. ponticum	E	2·5–6 m 8–20 ft	S.E. Europe, S.W. Asia	c. 1780

Some of my remarks regarding the Cherry Laurel are equally true of the Pontic Rhododendron, the only species that behaves like a real native in these islands. It forms an impenetrable thicket and its branches root as they lie on the ground; in addition it seeds itself freely. The Pontic Rhododendron varies much in the wild and in addition to this many plants throughout Britain are probably hybrids, often with *R. catawbiense* or *R. maximum*.

Though introduced about two hundred years later than the laurel, during the late eighteenth century and during the nineteenth and early twentieth centuries it was planted in quantity, at one time to provide game covert. From a landscape point of view it will quickly provide a green understorey to woodland on lime-free soil. The fact that it is always raised from seed results in varied growth coupled with a display of blossom of varying tints over a long period. Being the species most usually employed as a grafting stock for garden varieties it is often maligned on account of the suckers it produces. But away from the reds and pinks it comes into its own with a soft lilac-pink or lilac-lavender which is quite unequalled for contrast with the fresh greens of early summer.

ROBINIA   False Acacia or Locust

Species	D/E	Approx. Height	Native Habitat	Date of Introduction
R. pseudacacia	D	21–25 m 70–80 ft	Eastern USA	c. 1630

A native of the United States, the False Acacia was introduced to Britain in the early seventeenth century. In the early nineteenth century William Cobbett extolled its virtues and was instrumental in its temporary adoption as a timber tree. It did not survive his art of persuasion, but remains a comparatively common tree in parks and gardens, thriving on sandy soils in the southern and eastern parts of Britain. It is easily raised from seed and spreads freely from suckers. Its main disadvantage is that its branches are brittle and easily broken by gales. Even so, in time the trees (which are very quick-growing when young) build up into fine specimens surviving into a gaunt and picturesque old age. Its white laburnum-like flowers are at once an advantage and a disadvantage in the landscape: they appear when the flowers of most trees are over, but they are rather outlandish and of a garden nature. Its greatest asset in the landscape is that its leaves do not appear until late spring or early summer, when their fresh greenery echoes the past spring's tender tints, and their pinnate shape, composed as they are of many small rounded lobes, provides a wonderful softness. On the whole this foreigner dissolves well into the near landscape, but is only to be recommended for an occasional planting or group. Large specimens may achieve 28 m (90 ft).

SALIX   Willow

Species	D/E	Approx. Height	Native Habitat	Date of Introduction
S. alba White Willow	D	18–25 m 60–80 ft	Europe (Britain), W. Asia	
S.a. 'Caerulea' Cricket Bat Willow	D	21–28 m 70–90 ft	Unknown origin	
S.a. argentea (*S.a. sericea* or *regalis*) Silver Willow	D	9–15 m 30–50 ft	Unknown origin	
S.a. 'Britzensis'	D	9–15 m 30–50 ft	Cultivated form	

S.a. vitellina Golden Willow	D	9–15 m 30–50 ft	Cultivated form	
S. fragilis Crack Willow	D	9–15 m 30–50 ft	Europe (Britain), Caucasus	1829
S. caprea Goat Willow or Great Sallow	D	3–9 m 10–30 ft	Europe (Britain), N.W. Asia	
S. daphnoides Violet Willow	D	6–9 m 20–30 ft	Europe (not Britain)	c. 1829
S. triandra	D	3–6 m 10–20 ft	Eurasia (Britain)	
S. viminalis Common Osier	D	3–6 m 10–20 ft	Asia, Europe and S. Britain	
S. × sepulchralis 'Chrysocoma' Golden Weeping Willow	D	12–15 m 40–50 ft	Hybrid	19th cent.
S. × sepulchralis 'Salamonii'	D	15–18 m 50–60 ft	Hybrid	1869

Among willows no native species makes so splendid a tree as the White Willow; it is moreover the largest of our willows. Though "majestic" is seldom applied to a willow, a really large specimen is entitled to this adjective. Erect of growth, making a large loose head, the lowest branches frequently hang gracefully and the masses of narrow leaves give a light sheen, silvery grey-green in colour, accentuated by bright light and the breeze. It has long been a popular tree in husbandry, being used to hold up river- and stream-banks and to provide timber for hurdles. For this purpose, to keep the young shoots out of the reach of cattle, it has been a favourite for pollarding. It is worth growing a male form because of the conspicuous, fragrant, yellow catkins. The Cricket Bat Willow is a more slender tree; partly because it concentrates its efforts vertically it is exceptionally fast-growing even for a willow. The foliage is a blue-green, and as it is a female tree the catkins are not conspicuous. The Silver Willow is a lesser tree of similar narrow outline, and slower growing. The dense covering of silvery hairs on the leaves makes it a conspicuous landscape tree; in the distance it looks almost white in bright light.

Some forms are noted for their yellow or bright orange-red winter bark; the most usual of the latter is 'Britzensis' which makes a comparatively slender tree, paint-brush shaped, dipped in bright paint. It can be seen lighting the winter landscape in many limy valleys in the Cotswolds and along the Test in Hampshire. (Other clones of similar colouring are *S.a. chermesina*, 'Chrysostella' and 'Cardinal'.) *S.a. vitellina* resembles 'Britzensis' in growth but the twigs are bright yellow. They are propagated in nurseries, vegetatively, from clones. In fact this applies to all willows and even old groups of the Crack Willow exhibit a uniformity of outline – close-cropped to the sky – which cannot go unnoticed. In winter the Crack Willow, and particularly the form or hybrid called 'Basfordiana', has twigs of bright khaki-orange; the summer foliage is a rich glossy green, silvery beneath; its male catkins are bright yellow and conspicuous. It is a valuable medium-sized bushy tree of dense growth to about 12 m (40 ft).

The Sallow or Goat Willow germinates freely everywhere from seed, exhibiting a wide range of growth and hybridity and producing both male trees (with brilliant yellow Pussy Willow catkins) and females (with grey-green catkins). In marshy ground it is invaluable for breaking up plantations of vegetatively propagated willows. The Grey Willow has similar characteristics but whereas the Sallow achieves 9 m (30 ft) or more the Grey Willow is usually a shrub. Both have grey undersides to the leaves.

The Violet Willow is a useful extra, with its slender growth, purplish bark covered with white "bloom", yellow catkins (male) and narrow dark green leaves, grey beneath. It is a rapid grower while young and then slows. *S. triandra*, a bushy low tree, has abundant yellow catkins on male clones.

The Common Osier is usually a bushy plant with ascending branches clad in long narrow leaves, dark green above but showing their grey undersides in every breeze. The catkins are not conspicuous. Many of the most popular basket-willows derive from this species and it is a useful addition to low-growing species for forming varied thickets.

There remain the weeping willows. They belong partly to the garden and partly to the landscape. The prospect of one or two anywhere gives an effect unlike any other tree, and so long as they are associated with water all is well. The most common is the Golden Weeping Willow, which in addition to the above name has also been known as *S. alba* 'Tristis', *S.a. vitellina pendula* and *S. babylonica ramulis aureis*. It is usually as wide as it is high and only exhibits its most weeping shape in valleys or out of the wind; in windy places it presents an untidy and rather shapeless appearance. The long yellow hanging twigs are a great delight in winter and the pale young foliage adds to the beauty of earliest spring. 'Salamonii' has greenish twigs and is a taller, narrower tree. It is probably more suited to the general landscape, while the Golden Weeping Willow is appropriate nearer to dwellings. Because of its numerous twigs the latter quickly makes a very good screen even in winter.

While all of the above willows will grow in marshy ground, the best disease-free growth usually results on trees planted in normal, drained soil, limy if possible. Willows as a whole are comparatively short-lived trees.

SAMBUCUS Elder

Species	D/E	Approx. Height	Native Habitat	Date of Introduction
S. nigra Common Elder	D	3–5·5 m 10–18 ft	Europe (Britain), N. Africa, S.W. Asia	
S. racemosa Red-berried Elder	D	2·5–3·8 m 8–12 ft	Europe, Asia Minor, Siberia, W. Asia	16th cent.

Whether the landowner likes it or not, the native Common Elder will probably find its way into plantings of all kinds as the berries are readily spread by the birds and so germinate freely. It has one possible use where no other shrub would be successful, and that is as a screen under yews on chalky soil.

The Red-berried Elder is not a native but acts like one in the north of England and the Lowlands of Scotland. It is a more erect shrub with creamy flower heads like those of the Common Elder, followed by bunches of scarlet berries in late summer.

SORBUS Rowan, Whitebeam and Service Tree

Species	D/E	Approx. Height	Native Habitat	Date of Introduction
S. aria Whitebeam	D	9–15 m 30–50 ft	Europe (S. England)	
S. aucuparia Rowan or Mountain Ash	D	9–15 m 30–50 ft	Europe (Britain), Asia	
S. torminalis Wild Service Tree	D	9–12 m 30–40 ft	Europe (England), S.W. Asia, N. Africa	
S. domestica Service Tree	D	12–18 m 40–60 ft	S. and E. Europe, Causasus, N. Africa	

Apart from the Hawthorn and Field Maple there is no tree so characteristic for our chalky uplands – and indeed for better soils and conditions – when we are looking for a small-growing species, as the Whitebeam and its variants. Fortunately it is often raised from seed and so is suitable for landscape planting, whereas its forms, variants and hybrids are not. They are trees for gardens and arboreta, not for the landscape.

The Whitebeam makes a dense head which brings into prominence the silvery grey of the opening leaves; the trees can be picked out at a great distance in late spring. The leaves turn to dark greyish green for the summer, retaining to a variable degree their grey tint on the undersides. They turn brown in autumn, at which time bunches of dark red berries are produced. The Whitebeam keeps to its individual shape and does not make a united canopy. The Swedish Whitebeam, *S. intermedia*, is a tree of similar size and value and though normally raised from seeds is remarkably uniform. The Hawthorn, Whitebeam and Rowan are three genera of Rosaceous trees of great value for their small size in the landscape.

While the Whitebeam and the Hawthorn frequent limy uplands, the Rowan ascends to great height on acid hillsides in the north of England, and in Wales and Scotland, but is less common away from cultivated sites in the south. Following its white flowers in summer the bunches of brilliant scarlet fruits in August signal the approach of autumn; when the birds have taken the fruit the leaves turn to varied rich colours. It will thrive wherever it can get a roothold, and is a slender useful tree for the middle distance. Many Chinese and other species resemble it but unless seed-raised stock is obtainable – hybridised, no doubt – they should be avoided for landscape planting.

The two Service Trees are quite distinct: one is a native, the Wild Service Tree, while the other is a Southern European, the true Service Tree. The former has leaves with jagged lobes, almost maple-like, the latter pinnate leaves like those of a Rowan. They both excel in autumn colour and make a pleasing diversion to point out along drives, for instance, but are not sufficiently characterful for landscape planting, though they have similar assets to other species of *Sorbus* and enjoy the same conditions.

TAXUS   Yew

Species	D/E	Approx. Height	Native Habitat	Date of Introduction
T. baccata Common Yew	E	6–15 m 20–50 ft	Europe (Britain), N. Africa, W. Asia	

Although the Common or English Yew grows freely on chalky soils it thrives equally well on other limy formations and also on acid sands, in sun or shade. As a tree it can achieve more than 9 m (30 ft), and as likely as not some of the trunk, which has a dark reddish colour when wet, will be visible. Its principal contribution to the landscape is its dark greenery, produced by such small leaves that a velvety, *receding* effect is noticeable, and this is enhanced by shade. No other tree gives such a dark, dense appearance. Being shade-tolerant it is invaluable, with the holly, for filling in the understorey of woodlands, to act as a low screen. In spring the male trees bear multitudes of creamy yellow flowers which shed copious pollen; in the autumn the fleshy crimson fruits of the female trees are conspicuous, but neither display makes much effect at a distance. It is usually responsive to severe pruning, but the males are sometimes hesitant. The berries are poisonous. Care must be taken to see that animals do not eat the foliage, and dead foliage appears to be more harmful to cattle than live; in fact deer eat the live foliage with impunity. Used either in thin woodland or in the open it is one of the best permanent screens but is comparatively slow-growing.

At Wallington, Northumberland, in a district where small deer abound and had eaten away all low branches, an underplanting of *Lonicera nitida* (which deer do not eat) did much to improve the appearance of yews open to view. Golden yews eaten in the same way could be underplanted with *L.n.* 'Baggesen's Gold'. At a distance, across a wide lawn, such underplanting is scarcely noticeable.

THUJA   Arborvitae

Species	D/E	Approx. Height	Native Habitat	Date of Introduction
T. plicata (*T. gigantea*, *T. lobbii*) Western Red Cedar	E	18–38 m 60–130 ft	Western N. America	1853

This tree has taken nearly as well to our conditions as the Lawson's Cypress, and it is more successful on chalky soils. Its rapid growth when young and its rich fresh greenery serve to recommend it as a temporary screen, even in thin woodland. It retains a tapering conical form until old age and thus cannot be said to merge into our native woods as well as the Lawson's Cypress. In common with *Sequoia* and its relatives, we do not know what size it will achieve in these islands and, with them, it is best left to the arboreta and valley planting.

TILIA   Lime

Species	D/E	Approx. Height	Native Habitat	Date of Introduction
T. × europaea (*T. vulgaris*) Common Lime	D	28–38 m 90–120 ft	Hybrid	
T. platyphyllos Broad-leafed Lime	D	28–38 m 90–120 ft	Europe (Britain), S.W. Asia	

Species	D/E	Approx. Height	Native Habitat	Date of Introduction
T. platyphyllos 'Rubra' or 'Corallina' Red-twig Lime	D	28–38 m 90–120 ft		
T. cordata Small-leafed Lime	D	18–28 m 60–90 ft	Europe (Britain), Caucasus	
T. tomentosa (*T. argentea*) European White Lime	D	21–30 m 70–100 ft	S.E. Europe	1767
T. 'Petiolaris' Pendent White Lime	D	25–38 m 80–120 ft	Hybrid	c. 1840

The one thing that all limes have in common is the heady fragrance of the flowers. In most species it occurs at the crown of the year – the junction of June and July – when warmth and growth combine to attract the most insects, and we are more likely to enjoy the fragrance which is so freely borne in the air. The majority of species have a similar sweet scent, but the European White Lime, its hybrids and some relatives, all of which inherit to some extent the grey undersides to the leaves, flower in August, presenting the smell of a field of Red Clover. While most limes are perfectly suitable for mixing in plantations or using singly, wherever possible they should be brought near to the dwelling or focal point and planted all around it so that whichever way the wind blows some fragrance will be apparent.

Limes native to Britain are the Small-leafed and the Broad-leafed, and they are two very good species. Unfortunately the so-called Common Lime, a hybrid between the two, found favour with early nurserymen, particularly in Holland. It is "Common" merely because it was the kind most commonly planted. Old avenues still exist from the seventeenth century causing much work if the masses of adventitious shoots from the trunk – noticeably at the base – are to be kept under control. Though early in leaf it is early in losing its leaves, and during the summer is prone (like its parents) to severe attacks of aphides which make everything beneath it sticky. It makes a handsome, free- and rapid-growing tree when young but in old age dies from the top downwards and becomes thin and gaunt. Whether the fact that it produced so many adventitious shoots recommended it to the early nurserymen for propagation by layering, or whether this characteristic developed from increased propagation by layering, cannot be told. It is a sterile hybrid. In any event, while we inherit many avenues of it – of historic value – it should not be planted or propagated except to retain a few specimens in arboreta.

The Small-leafed Lime in Shugborough Park, Staffordshire (National Trust). It is considered by many to be the best substitute for the English Elm. Its creamy flowers are borne above the twigs and create a marked effect in July.

There is no doubt that the most popular lime for general ornamental planting today – and indeed the most popular for most of the twentieth century – is the Broad-leafed Lime. Avenues of this species perhaps now outnumber those of the Common Lime, under which name it is often erroneously found. For avenue planting the vegetatively propagated true Red-twig Lime 'Rubra' or 'Corallina' is often preferred, if obtainable, since it produces uniform growth, but it is less vigorous than normal trees of the species raised from seeds. (Although this richly tinted clone has been named 'Rubra', *T. platyphyllos* itself has winter twigs of markedly reddish green, giving a rich tone in the mass.) Obviously the seed-raised trees are the best for clumps and small and large woodlands. It thrives on many, in fact most, soils, but is most luxuriant on a deep loam, preferably limy. Some errant trees raised from seeds produce sprouting shoots at the base; because it is often used as a stock for grafting other limes this can at times be a nuisance, but the sprouts are never so prevalent as in the Common Lime. It forms a stately tree with usually a somewhat conical head; it leafs early, flowers freely in late June, and develops its autumn colour and loses its leaves early in the autumn. Occasionally low branches take root and a thicket of stems ascends.

A group of Small-leafed Lime near Yelverton in Devon. At a distance they could easily be mistaken for English Elms.

Though the Broad-leafed Lime may be the commonest lime planted today, another native species, the Small-leafed Lime is by far the most valuable for general landscape planting. While the Broad-leafed Lime has large leaves and drooping flowers, the Small-leafed tree has comparatively small leaves and the flowers are borne conspicuously above them; each species thus has a distinct appearance. The Small-leafed Lime forms tall dignified specimens, on a par with our greater natives, with large rounded crowns and in winter a greenish mass of twigs. The flowers open slightly later than those of the Broad-leafed Lime. There is no doubt that this tree, usually seed-raised, is among the best reasonably quick-growing substitutes for the English Elm. In maturity it is a tree of considerable majesty. Unfortunately many of the stocks raised by nurserymen are propagated from seeds or cuttings from mixed strains. Seeds should only be used from major stands in Europe where there is little chance of hybrids occurring.

These three limes suffer from aphides which cause a sticky drip, and are therefore best kept away from garden and car-park areas.

There are many other good limes but since they are all vegetatively propagated they are not to be recommended for landscape planting except in the foreground, to link the greater trees to the dwelling. Two are of great size, the European White Lime and its supposed hybrid the Pendent White Lime; the latter will frequently ascend to 28 m (90 ft) or more. Both have grey undersides to the leaf and do not attract aphides; on the other hand their pollen is poisonous to bumble bees. The European White Lime forms a very wide head of rather ascending branches, while the Pendent White Lime, often called the Silver Weeping Lime, is taller, narrower and more arching. In parkland conditions it can dominate all but the very largest of trees. They both flower in August with a fragrance of Red Clover. These two species' leaves turn yellow in autumn, and when fallen on the ground exhibit a delightful pattern of yellow mixed with the grey reverses. The Pendent White Lime is a conspicuous individual and should be used sparingly.

Two other small, July-flowering, non-poisonous limes are *T. euchlora* and *T. oliveri*, the former a slender bright green tree, the latter wide-spreading with grey undersurfaces to the leaves. They are suitable for small avenues, and foreground planting. They are not subject to aphis attacks, although *T. euchlora* has, of late years, suffered increasingly from a disease of the bark, and so cannot be thoroughly recommended. Together with the greater limes, there is a wide range of types and sizes, enough to enable planting to be done particularly around habitable areas, to gain the benefit of the fragrance of the flowers.

Tsuga   Hemlock Spruce

Species	D/E	Approx. Height	Native Habitat	Date of Introduction
T. heterophylla Western Hemlock	E	30–60 m 100–200 ft	Western N. America	1851
T. canadensis Eastern Hemlock	E	18–28 m 60–90 ft	Eastern N. America	early 18th cent.

The Western Hemlock is a much quicker grower than the Eastern and is used extensively for forestry. It is an invaluable crop for acid, sandy and loamy soils and is invariably slender and graceful. Its eventual great height and tapering apex – at least up to the present in Britain – precludes it as a landscape tree but it has great value for temporary or long-term screening since, *if well spaced*, it retains its lowest branches indefinitely.

The Eastern Hemlock was introduced earlier, but in view of the Western species' splendid growth, both as a slender graceful conifer and as a forestry crop, it has been considerably neglected as an amenity tree. It will grow in drier conditions than the Western species and will also tolerate lime. It is in addition one of the few conifers which develop several stems and produce a rounded crown, thus assorting well with Scots Pine and the others we have selected. Tsugas should be planted when quite small.

ULMUS Elm

Species	D/E	Approx. Height	Native Habitat	Date of Introduction
U. procera (*U. campestre*) English Elm	D	28–30·8 m 90–120 ft	England	
U. glabra (*U. montana*) Wych or Scotch Elm	D	25–30 m 80–100 ft	Europe (Britain)	
U. angustifoliia (*U. stricta*) *cornubiense* Cornish Elm	D	28–30 m 80–100 ft	Cornwall, S.W. England	
U. carpinifolia (*U. nitens*) Smooth-leafed Elm	D	25–30 m 80–100 ft	Europe (E. England), N. Africa, S.W. Asia	

We do not know the future of elms in Britain. Perhaps the beetle will die out and our landscape will again, in a hundred years' time, be enriched in the lowlands by the majestic English Elm, and elsewhere by the grace of the Wych Elm. All elms produce tiny leaves in spring of a vivid green and most turn to bright yellow in autumn; in addition their pre-leafing purplish flowers give a warm tone to the landscape in March. In the hope that some will prosper we should plant elms and foster young suckers in the hedgerows.

Most hedgerow suckers are of the English Elm, which is a common tree on good deep soil through the shires and into Devon. Its origin is not known and probably, being almost sterile, it was spread from field boundary to field boundary. The much less majestic but far more graceful Wych Elm replaces it in the north and west and is a fairly freely seeding tree. It is specially valuable, like the Sycamore, in hilly country, but develops its greatest size and beauty on good land. In the far south-west the stalwart, upright (almost conical) forms of the Cornish Elm replace the others, and are very characteristic in the landscape. Another narrow tree is found in East Anglia, the Smooth-leafed Elm, a graceful tree often of slight quality. (The nomenclature of the last two is very confusing if one goes into details.) These roughly outlined districts indicate the choice that should be made for soils and conditions. Though nothing equals the upstanding port and cumulus-headed majesty of the English Elm, the round-headed – very variable – Wych Elm is not to be despised and has a totally different set of values. The clean fresh green of the young spring foliage is eclipsed in early summer, particularly in the Wych Elm, by the development of the light green samaras, giving another touch of spring's freshness.

There is a series of hybrids from *U. glabra*, named *U. × hollandica*, the most notable example being 'Vegeta', the Huntingdon or Chichester Elm. It inherits the best characteristics of the Wych Elm in its lofty rapid growth, its large leaves followed by plentiful though sterile samaras, and consistent yellow autumn colour. It is, however, propagated vegetatively and is therefore best used as an avenue tree, where uniform growth is an asset, and only very occasional use in park planting is acceptable.

VIBURNUM

Species	D/E	Approx. Height	Native Habitat	Date of Introduction
V. lantana Wayfaring Tree	D	2·5–2·8 m 8–12 ft	Europe (England), Middle East	
V. opulus Guelder Rose	D	3·5–3·8 m 8–12 ft	Europe (Britain), Middle East	

Although these two well-known shrubs will grow well on any reasonable, drained soil, they are particularly useful for chalk. The Wayfaring Tree has heads of small white flowers followed by red berries turning black in late summer and good autumn colour. The Guelder Rose is much more showy in flower, in its autumn colour and in its bunches of shining scarlet berries. Both shrubs have an offensive smell throughout the year and should therefore be kept away from dwellings.

The avenue of Huntingdon Elms at Hidcote, Gloucestershire (National Trust). It succumbed to the elm disease and has been replaced by limes and Turkey Oaks. Much skill had gone into the pruning of the fifty-year-old trees to achieve the gothic arch effect.

6

AVENUES

Shadowy aisles of pillared trees
Now my errant fancy please,
Dim cathedral walks like these;
Nave by numerous transepts crost,
Each in his own long darkness lost.

George Darley (1795–1846)

The word "avenue" simply means "the way of approach" and what more natural than that it should be marked by a row of stakes? And if those stakes happened to grow, they would form trees bordering the way, at least on one side. Or if the way were cut out of woodland or open forest, the trees left would equally well mark the route. Avenues had their great period of fashion in England in the seventeenth century, derived from their popularity in France, where on some of the flatter land around Paris they were a triumphant success, marching through clearing and woodland alike. Their very length obscured defects such as the failure of trees in certain spots. In England the fashion grew speedily after the Restoration. Some avenues were no doubt cut through woodland, but probably as many were actually planted, and this was for a variety of reasons. One was that the English nurserymen were beginning to produce quantities of trees; until then, as far as one can gather, the cutting down of trees and the making of clearances were common and the replacement of trees was not taken seriously until John Evelyn strove to call attention to the decreasing woodlands. There was a general imposing of man's will on the landscape, a proliferation of tree-lined vistas from the great houses of the nobility, and the added discovery that looking down a long vista appeared to increase its length, whereas looking upwards to a house tended to belittle the building. All this could be exaggerated by false perspectives, and, in more intimate areas, by the use of the *trompe l'œil*.

Our avenues are frequently the relics of formality left to us from the pre-Repton centuries, such as at Ashdown, Oxfordshire, and Lyme Park, Cheshire. These are both focused on the house. At Blickling, Norfolk, at Hardwick Hall, Derbyshire, and at Anglesey Abbey, Cambridgeshire, they are progressively younger and lead us in thought to the parkland beyond.

The remains of an old avenue at Ham House, London, moves from the great gates across to Ham Common, but when the new length of limes just beyond the gates was planted it was not aligned exactly on the gate piers! Owing to the proximity of a wall on one side it is doubtful whether it will ever be corrected.

The most popular trees for planting in avenues were those which grew well and could be produced quickly and in quantity. It was easy to raise beech trees and chestnuts from seeds; oaks also grow well from seeds but are slow in growth in early years. The English Elm is prolific of its underground suckers, but like many plants with this propensity, it seldom produces seeds. Today, quite apart from the dreadful loss of millions of trees through disease, it is seldom seen as a woodland tree, but nearly always in hedgerows. This can be attributed not only to its ease of rooting and readiness to be transplanted to make a boundary, but also to its liking for good deep soil which would already have been cleared for farming. The Lombardy Poplar,

A very broad avenue of Horse Chestnuts at Blickling Hall, Norfolk (National Trust).

An informal avenue of Turkey Oaks, planted in broken clumps, in the approach to Hardwick Hall, Derbyshire (National Trust).

so beloved in France, was not introduced into Britain until too late for the fashion for avenues. The lime has, however, always been the most popular tree for avenues, partly on account of its fragrant flowers and partly because the Dutch had found that the Common Lime was easy to reproduce from its prolific basal shoots. (It is open to question whether this is the *cause* of this unfortunate habit, perpetuated over hundreds of years.) It is a sterile hybrid between the Small-leafed Lime and the Broad-leafed Lime.

It is normal for trees to grow in close proximity to others. Although they produce very handsome specimens when grown singly in conditions to their liking, they do not really give of their best in exposed windy positions. We are apt to judge trees by single specimens, not by attenuated trees in woodland, where, closely pressed by their neighbours, they tend to develop tall stems and small heads. This is exactly what the Common Lime does,

The avenue of limes at Tatton Park, Cheshire (National Trust), interspersed with beeches and sycamores, planted at the end of the eighteenth century. The trees show the browsing line made by deer.

whether grown singly or as an avenue. Perhaps this is why it was so popular, but I think its uniformity from being vegetatively propagated, especially by the astute businessmen of Holland, was a factor of equal importance. Whatever may have been the reason, the Common Lime was almost always the tree used in very old avenues. With today's shortage of labour we do not use it, mainly because of its prolific basal shoots which have to be cut away every winter, or treated with a hormone growth-inhibitor. Sometimes these basal shoots are clipped into a sort of basal hedge below the avenue, as at Hopetoun House, Lothian.

With the advent of the landscape movement of the eighteenth century, avenues became outmoded, and also the use of the Common Lime, whose

The double avenue of limes which stretches for three miles through Clumber Park, Nottinghamshire (National Trust). Here the trees have been trimmed out of reach of animals. The trees were planted just before the middle of the nineteenth century.

A wide avenue of English Oaks, near Elstead, Surrey.

This avenue of Sweet or Spanish Chestnuts is about 350 years old. At Croft Castle, Herefordshire (National Trust).

narrow outline was useless for the comfortable contours desired of specimen trees. William Kent still used avenues, although to Capability Brown they were anathema. Humphry Repton allowed them as long as they were not straight, and indeed it was on his recommendation that one of the country's longest avenues – double rows of Common Lime which wind their way for three miles through Clumber Park – was planted in 1840. As a rule he subscribed to the precept that turns and twists should follow the contours of the land, and are not usually acceptable on flat ground. *Tilia platyphyllos* at times develops a narrow outline and has been increasingly used as an avenue tree since the late nineteenth century. *Tilia cordata* reliably makes a fine rounded crown and a number of isolated trees in our parks prove its

Narrowly and closely planted beech trees in the garden avenue at Hidcote, Gloucestershire (National Trust), before thinning.

An avenue of Lombardy Poplars at Madresfield Court, Worcestershire.

popularity – due in part, no doubt, to its being so much more conspicuous when in flower than any other species, because it bears its flowers above the branchlets instead of hanging from them. Magnificent specimens may be seen at Clumber Park and Shugborough. Avenues are best on flat land where the soil does not vary much. Nothing is so disappointing as to see an avenue conceived with a good purpose, only to have that purpose defeated by inequality of growth. This is borne out by the avenue of Horse Chestnuts at Anglesey Abbey, Cambridgeshire. The trees, all planted at the same time, are twice as large at one end as they are at the other, because of greater fertility and moisture at the far end. Similar troubles arose at Buscot Park, Oxfordshire, where the late Lord Faringdon planted an avenue of Fastigiate

The historic avenue of beeches within the garden at Killerton, Devon (National Trust). As old trees fall, young trees are planted.

The dramatic line of Lombardy Poplars by the side of the mill-race, in the garden at Anglesey Abbey, Cambridgeshire, a property of the National Trust.

Oaks. The varying subsoil and drainage over the uneven terrain resulted in irregular growth, and the problem was compounded by the fact that two types of trees – some narrow and some broad – had become mixed in the nursery whence the stock was obtained. It is most important to study the water-table and also the subsoil over the entire length before planting.

If we think that the first avenues were the outcome of a row of stakes which took root, or forest clearance, or the deliberate planting of trees, we next come to the orderly mind which inaugurated planting at regular intervals. Only in this way can the avenue exert its tempting power to lead us along; we need to be made to feel a compulsion to get to the end to see what is there. It may be an object, or an open view. The terminus – no less than the beginning and length of the avenue – dictates its most suitable

152

width. Repton sounds a warning: "If at the end of a long avenue be placed an obelisk, or temple, or any other eye-trap, ignorance or childhood alone will be caught or pleased by it: . . . for this reason an avenue is most pleasing, which . . . climbs up a hill, and passing over its summit, leaves the fancy to conceive its termination." The second point in Repton's mind was that it takes someone who has some knowledge of trees and their growth to decide on the planting of an avenue, for there are many things to be considered, apart from the suitability of trees to the local soil and conditions.

The trees must be so placed in their rows that they have enough light and space to allow good growth. The rows must be placed wide enough apart for the same purpose. These are the practical considerations, after which it is a matter of aesthetics. While an avenue should lead to something, as I have said, and on that something depends its width, we should also think of the normal width of the tree chosen. Extreme measures produce the very narrow Gothic-arch effect, in an avenue where trees of normal growth are planted in lines close together, or an open V-shape, where the same trees are so spaced that with normal growth each can develop into a specimen. The pitfall with the narrower spacing is that for the first fifty years or so the view along the avenue will be closed by overlapping branches, unless they are high-clipped after the French fashion, or until the under branches can be pruned away, accelerating the natural production of the pointed arch.

Any effect can be achieved by the use of the right plants, at the right spacing. As a general rule we might expect to find a wide view approached by a wide avenue, a substantial vase or statue by a broad arch, an obelisk by a narrow one and a house perhaps by trees so spaced that their branches sweep the ground. Two exceptionally wide avenues are at Montacute, Somerset, where the conditions and spacing allow continual patching, and at Wimpole Hall, Cambridgeshire. Here the original avenue, being almost entirely of elms, has gone but has been replaced with *Tilia* × *europaea*.

If the planner of a new avenue has plenty to think about, conundrums of a different kind plague those of us who are faced with decaying avenues, and have to decide how they can be replaced. An avenue properly spaced originally is impossible to replace effectively except by clear-felling, and this is not always possible nor desirable. If the avenue has been given the right width – according to the objective to be reached – and the spacing between trees correctly chosen to give the desired proportion, there are four alternatives. One is to patch with the same species as trees become unsafe or fall; another is to fell alternate trees in the rows and replant at once choosing a species which is shade-tolerant; another is to clear-fell and start again, and the fourth is to let nature take its course with the old avenue and start another elsewhere in the meantime. There is seldom a plain answer; every avenue needs separate and expert appraisal. For the first expedient we need to gauge the life of the remaining trees, to ascertain that the patching will

result in a good and fairly uniform avenue in fifty to a hundred years. The second and third expedients are shocking to many because numerous trees will still be in their prime; the whole subject is emotive in the extreme. The fourth is not as easy as it sounds. It brings us to some fundamental questions: first, is the avenue in the right place and does it fulfil a function; secondly, is the tree chosen the right species for the position and the avenue's proportions; and thirdly, is there another site which needs an avenue? Repton was in two minds about avenues, as I indicated in Chapter 1. To his way of thinking, an avenue frequently cut a property in two, and a straight line was in any case foreign to a landscape. By breaking the avenue into clumps and single trees he opened cross views with considerable results, while still perhaps retaining enough trees to allow the semblance of an avenue to remain to lead the eye towards the distant object or view.

Today our avenues do not approach the length and majesty of those of the seventeenth and early eighteenth centuries, nor, with much of the landscape open, is there any need for them. They are usually planted nowadays along the approach to the dwelling and in some places, where the drive roughly follows the boundary of the property, they act as a useful screen or protection from neighbouring buildings or winds. Perhaps their greatest value today is in new towns or large housing estates, where amid a welter of curving roads and informal placing of dwellings a good straight avenue would have a sobering impact. This was particularly apparent when I assessed the planting schemes for the new townscape at Redditch. One good straight line – an avenue perhaps – through the middle would have pulled together the meandering roads and the constant changes of frontage. The planners were not afraid of straight lines when laying out Welwyn Garden City.

And so I suggest that, once we have thought seriously and concluded that an avenue is desirable, we have next to decide on the width and effect desired, and to suit these requirements by choosing the type of tree – and doing everything possible to ensure that their growth will be regular. This is partly governed by the soil and partly by the plants themselves. Our big native trees are all raised from seeds and the growth of individual specimens will naturally vary; therefore seeds from a good strain are advisable. Trees propagated vegetatively are usually more uniform in growth, especially when grown from cuttings. If they are grafted, their stocks will vary in vigour. When choosing a species of tree for an avenue it is worth walking down the Pagoda Vista at Kew, where there are many different trees placed opposite each other in pairs, so that the results of different combinations in regard to placing and shape can be gauged.

Above left, the beech avenue at Springhill, planted c. 1700 by Good Will Conyngham but later lost. Below, the trees were replaced by his descendant, Mrs Diana McClintock (née Lennox-Conyngham), c. 1969.

7

TODAY'S AFTERTHOUGHTS

From the St Lawrence Valley and the Canadian Lakes southward to the Allegheny Mountains there is displayed each autumn a scene of entrancing beauty not surpassed the world over. Central Europe, Japan, China and other parts of eastern Asia have their own season of autumn color and each area has its individuality but, if they rival, they cannot surpass the forest scenes of eastern North America.

Ernest H. Wilson, *Aristocrats of the Garden* (1937)

While it is perfectly permissible and even advisable to apply Repton's ideals and maxims to the countryside in general and to eighteenth- and early-nineteenth-century park landscapes, I think they can also be applied to designs of more recent times because the beauty of our humanised landscapes has never been surpassed. Repton died in 1818. During the rest of the century, and indeed into the twentieth, many things happened which completely altered the eighteenth-century way of life and its outlook. We conveniently bring in Queen Victoria's accession in 1837 as a useful date; this was also the period of J. C. Loudon's *Encyclopaedia of Gardening*, Joseph Paxton's activities in many parts of the country, the impending Industrial Revolution and the arrival in ever greater numbers of trees from foreign countries of both the Northern and Southern Hemispheres, most of which have proved amenable to our climate. The new estates owned by the business magnates might be smaller than those of the great landowners, but they needed designing and planting. There was a great upsurge in botanical study of the new trees and plant life in general. The paupers of industry in the new towns needed open spaces for recreation and the Public Health Act of 1848 led to many historic public parks being laid out. During the early Victorian era there was a completely new look at the countryside in and around the fast-expanding towns. Later, in the course of the twentieth century, the movement spread to garden cities, playing fields, factory sites, and the landscaping of motorways.

The question of the industrial world's approach to creating a landscape would provide material for a whole book and I hope it may be written soon, before the last Victorian touches have vanished. But it would not be right to finish this book without a brief review of such developments, principally because we need to have an understanding of what has happened before we can consider any new planting in public parks and like places.

I have made it clear that this is not a gardening book, but we cannot ignore the influence of J.C. London, who was not only much more of a gardener than a landscape gardener, but also coined the term 'gardenesque'. By this he intended a large garden or small park which should be devoted to a collection of beautiful and interesting trees, shrubs and plants, to which access should be freely available for studying them. This necessitated threading the area with paths, sometimes straight but often curved, which was an entirely new concept. This is the fundamental idea governing the design of all our public parks and garden cities and indeed most private gardens of the present day.

The first sign of any reaction to the new gardening, which included beds for exotics on the lawn, came from William Robinson. Through his writings he wielded as great an influence as Loudon. He had been to Paris and studied the magnificent new vistas and parks, and sought to influence Parliament to rethink the plan of London. This was not all: he was strongly against geometrical beds of garish flowers on the lawn, and venerated the beauty of trees and shrubs growing in natural conditions. His views are fully set out in his most famous book, *The English Flower Garden and Home Grounds*, first published in 1883 but reprinted in numerous editions to the present day. Though it is fairly obvious that his delight was in the plants themselves, he also concerned himself with the larger issues of landscape planting. Part of the introduction to one of his later books forms the epigraph to this present volume. Never were words so truly used. And this brings us directly to the modifying influence of Gertrude Jekyll . . .

I have indulged my fancies gently with the inclusion of some foreign trees in Chapter 5 but now I think it worth while to provide a short list of foreign deciduous trees, many of which blend admirably in our more formal landscapes. Their leaves and stance are all good but in addition to the conspicuous flowers that many produce, their principal contribution (apart from greenery) is autumn leaf-colour. Our natives give a warmth of yellows and russets in November, but many of these foreigners are far more brilliant and contribute their quota in October.

In the gardenesque designs, where every plant is an interesting specimen, the trim-looking conifers are much at home. These include the Wellingtonia, *Sequoia sempervirens*, *Cryptomeria japonica*, various eastern *Chamaecyparis*, *Cupressus*, *Abies*, *Picea*, *Pinus* and *Juniperus*, and many more but information regarding these stately trees I must leave you to seek else-where. They form the backbone of many arboreta and their inclusion here would overbalance this book which is really about reinstatement of earlier landscapes.

Here, then, is a list of trees, mainly deciduous, which should certainly be among those selected for the gardenesque landscapes; it will be noted that most of them have been in cultivation in Britain for a long time. To them can be added some of the exotics in Chapter 5.

Species	D/E*	Approx. Height	Native Habitat	Date Intro-duced	Comments
Acer cappadocicum (*A. laetum, A. colchicum*) Cappadocian Maple	D	15-18 m 50-60 ft	Caucasus to Asia Minor	1838	Excellent autumn colour; densely branching; produces suckers
A. palmatum Japanese Maple	D	6-15 m 20-50 ft	Japan, China, Korea	1820	Slow growing, autumn colour; red "keys"
A. macrophyllum Oregon Maple	D	18-25 m 60-80 ft	Western N. America	1827	Compact; large leaves; autumn colour
A. rubrum Red Maple	D	18-25 m 60-80 ft	Eastern N. America	c.1650	Red flowers in spring; autumn colour
A. saccharinum (*A. dasycarpum*) Silver Maple	D	25-30 m 80-100 ft	Eastern N. America	1725	Fast-growing, rather brittle; leaves nearly white beneath; autumn colour
A. saccharum Sugar Maple	D	15-21 m 50-70 ft	Eastern N. America	1735	Slow-growing autumn colour
Aesculus indica Indian Horse Chestnut	D	15-25 m 50-80 ft	N. India	1851	Compact, round-headed; light pink flowers in June; easily damaged by spring frosts
A. turbinata Japanese Horse Chestnut	D	15-25 m 50-80 ft	Japan	1880	Slow-growing; extra large leaves

* Deciduous or evergreen

Species	D/E	Approx. Height	Native Habitat	Date Introduced	Comments
Ailanthus altissima (*A. glandulosa*) Tree of Heaven	D	18-25 m 60-80 ft	N. China	1751	Ash-like leaves; produces suckers; bunches of reddish "keys" on females in late summer
Betula ermanii	D	15-25 m 50-80 ft	Eastern Asia	1890	Buff-coloured bark; strong-growing; autumn colour
B. nigra River Birch	D	9-15 m 30-50 ft	Eastern USA	1736	Brown, peeling bark; graceful open head; autumn colour
B. papyrifera Canoe or Paper Birch	D	15-18 m 50-60 ft	N. America	1750	Open-headed; white bark, often unblemished; autumn colour
Catalpa bignonioides (*C. syringaefolia*) Indian Bean	D	9-15 m 30-50 ft	Eastern USA	1726	Wide-spreading; large leaves and panicles of Horse Chestnut-like flowers in late summer
C. speciosa Western Catalpa	D	12-21 m 40-70 ft	Eastern USA	1880	Upright growth; large leaves; flowers earlier than *C. bignonioides*
Celtis occidentalis Hackberry	D	12-15 m 40-50 ft	USA	1656	Some autumn colour; black fruits
Cladrastis lutea (*Virgilia lutea*) Yellow Wood	D	9-15 m 30-50 ft	S. Eastern USA	1812	Small white flowers in hanging racemes; yellow autumn colour
Corylus colurna Turkish Hazel	D	18-21 m 60-70 ft	S.E. Europe Asia Minor	1582	Pyramid-shaped; long catkins
Diospyros virginiana Persimmon	D	12-18 m 40-60 ft	Eastern USA	1629	Autumn colour; plant female trees for fruit

Species	D/E	Approx. Height	Native Habitat	Date Introduced	Comments
Fagus sylvatica purpurea Purple Beech	D	21-30 m 70-100 ft	Switzerland	c.1760	Coppery purple foliage, autumn colour; 'Riversii', c.1870, usually preferred
F. s. 'Asplenifolia' Fern-leafed Beech	D	18-28 m 60-90 ft		1804	Dense head; autumn colour
Fraxinus ornus Manna Ash	D	12-18 m 40-60 ft	S. Europe, Asia Minor	early 18th cent.	White flowers in summer; dark autumn colour
Ginkgo biloba Maidenhair Tree	D	15-25 m 50-80 ft	W. China	1758	Somewhat pyramidal; autumn colour
Halesia monticola Mountain Snowdrop Tree	D	18-25 m 60-80 ft	Eastern USA	c.1897	White bell-flowers in spring; taller than *H. carolina*
Juglans nigra Black walnut	D	25-30 m 80-100 ft	E. and Central USA	early 17th cent.	Large, open head; ash-like leaves; hard nuts
J. regia Common Walnut	D	18-28 m 60-90 ft	S.E. Europe to Eastern Asia	long ago	Good winter silhouette; similar value to ash in landscape
Koelreuteria paniculata	D	9-18 m 30-60 ft	China	1763	Spring and autumn colour; panicles of small yellow flowers in late summer; green bladder-like pods
Laurus nobilis Bay Laurel	E	6-12 m 20-40 ft	Mediterranean Region	16th cent.	For our warmest counties
Liquidambar styraciflua Sweet Gum	D	18-25 m 60-80 ft	Eastern USA, Mexico	17th cent.	Autumn colour; best in deep, moist, acid soils
Liriodendron tulipifera Tulip Tree	D	25-38 m 80-110 ft	Eastern N. America	c.1650	Imposing; large leaves, yellowish flowers; autumn colour; not for chalk

Species	D/E	Approx. Height	Native Habitat	Date Introduced	Comments
Magnolia acuminata Cucumber Tree	D	15-21 m 50-70 ft	Eastern N. America	1736	Small, greenish-yellow flowers; large leaves
Nyssa sylvatica Tupelo, Black Gum	D	18-25 m 60-80 ft	Eastern N. America	early 18th cent.	Very fine red autumn colour in best forms
Oxydendrum arboreum Sorrel Tree	D	12-15 m 40-50 ft	Eastern N. America	1752	Small white bell-flowers in late summer; autumn colour
Phillyrea latifolia	E	3-6 m 10-20 ft	S. and E. Mediter-ranean	16th cent.	Small leaves; rounded head
Pterocarya fraxinifolia Caucasian Wing-nut	D	25-30 m 80-100 ft	Caucasus and North Persia	1782	Ash-like leaves; produces suckers; thrives in damp soil
Quercus coccinea Scarlet Oak	D	18-25 m 60-80 ft	Eastern N. America	end 17th cent.	Compact head; autumn colour; sandy soils best
Quercus × hispanica Lucombe Oak	E	25-30 m 80-100 ft	Hybrid	c.1763	*Q. cerris × Q. suber*; Large rounded head; semi-evergreen
Q. palustris Pin Oak	D	21-28 m 70-90 ft	Eastern USA	1800	Graceful head; autumn colour; rapid growth
Q. rubra Red Oak	D	18-25 m 60-80 ft	Eastern N. America	early 18th cent.	Rapid growth; wide, rounded head; young leaves yellow; autumn colour
Q. virginiana Live Oak	E	9 m 30 ft	S.E. USA, N.E. Mexico W. Cuba	1739	Wide-spreading
Sassafras albidum	D	15-21 m 50-70 ft	Eastern and Central USA	c.1630	Strangely lobed leaves; autumn colour
Taxodium distichum Swamp Cypress	D	28-38 m 90-120 ft	Eastern USA	c.1640	Conical; feathery leaves; autumn colour; moist or wet soil
Umbellularia californica Californian Laurel	E	9-15 m 30-50 ft	Western USA	1826	For our warmer counties
Zelkova carpinifolia	D	25-30 m 80-100 ft	S.E. Asia	c.1780	Vase-shaped; small leaves; autumn colour
Z. serrata Keaki	D	15-21 m 50-70 ft	Japan, Formosa, etc.	1861	Wide-spreading; autumn colour

8

THE LANDSCAPE OF THE GARDEN

For gardens ... ought ... to be divided into three parts; a green in the entrance, a heath, or desert in the going forth, and the main garden in the midst. The green hath two pleasures: the one, because nothing is more pleasant to the eye than green grass kept finely shorn; the other because it will give you a fair alley in the midst.

Sir Francis Bacon (1561–1626)

I have, I think, made it clear that this is not a gardening book; however, I hope it will be read by gardeners as well as landscape planters. There are, after all, many gardens which depend for their success on the prospect over the landscape. In this chapter I intend to offer gardeners some general guidelines in the hope that some of the thoughts I put forward may be of use to those who wish to adapt the disciplines of my earlier chapters to the making of their gardens. The whole thing is summed up by two words: transition and suitability.

The question of transition involves the movement from the house to the garden and from the garden out into the landscape; suitability covers both the practical and aesthetic fitness of particular plants for local conditions of weather and soil, and in regard to architecture and landscaping.

Suiting the Plants to the Conditions

Whatever our preferences in plants may be, their choice is best considered after we have observed the "capabilities" of the house. All houses have a personality, some forceful and formal, others retiring and informal – or a combination of the two. It is the formal ones which suggest, even demand, a formal garden at least immediately around them. (This is strange when we remember that England's greatest period of informal garden design coincided with the building of the most formal dwellings.) Coupled with the choice of a formal or informal design to fit the house, the selection of plants needs careful thought. The key word is suitability. A would-be gardener usually already has some preferences in plants, but it is important to weigh these against their suitability or otherwise to the house and local conditions of soil and climate.

Many years ago I was asked to help design and plant a large garden which was principally to be composed of rhododendrons, azaleas, camellias and the like. When I arrived at the site I found a thin cover of pale grey soil overlying solid chalk. This is one of the first practical points to be considered: whether the soil is limy or not. The chalk forbade entirely the original choice of plants though a good selection of shrubs – species and varieties of *Viburnum, Philadelphus, Berberis, Hypericum, Mahonia* and others – in the end created an acceptable garden. The house was modern, of informal design and stood on undulating ground. An old Tudor house might be thought the ideal companion to a knot garden of herbs, but this has to be ruled out if the soil is wet clay. An acid, sandy soil would have suited all the lime-hating plants; the heavier soils are perfect for roses and most shrubs; a high water-table would be just right for moisture-lovers and dense shade is not impossible to cope with. Patterns of weather, not only the rainfall and prevailing wind but also extremes of temperature, must be studied. A friend who is a great gardener fell in love with a charming house but it was not until he had spent a few seasons there that he realised that, although its setting was beautiful and fertile, complete with a stream winding through well-drained soil, the tract of land was in a frost pocket. I may add that, though so keen a gardener, his love for the house has resulted in his staying in it, but his garden seldom escapes late spring frost damage.

Many folk hanker after water, but there is one golden rule which applies to its use and that is if it is to be informal or natural, it *must* be in the lowest part of the ground, whereas pools and canals of geometrical shape can be used effectively on any level.

These points bring out the fundamentals of gardening. We cannot escape Nature and all her manifold resources, against which we immediately pit our puny efforts the moment we start gardening – or, for that matter, farming. Whatever else we may desire, Nature, in the form of the capabilities of the site, must be considered first. I should add that even so there are many people who feel a certain triumph in defeating Nature; they are those whose love for plants makes them build up high beds of lime-free soil to accommodate lime-haters. (Lawrence Johnston used sawdust some sixty or more years ago at Hidcote to achieve this and it is surprising how successful the beds remain.) They get over the fact that their garden is on dry, freely drained soil by making artificial bog gardens with the aid of clay or sheets of Butyl. They build walls to shelter their tender plants, and even in the good old days constructed hollow walls which were heated through flues from without to hasten the ripening of peaches and pears in cold climates. They go to great lengths to drain a marshy piece of ground in order to grow roses and hardy flowers when it would be ideal, perhaps, for moisture-loving herbaceous plants and shrubs. They cut down trees and "open up" the garden when in reality the shade would give them a priceless opportunity to grow shade-lovers. This brings us to the basic fact that whatever our climate or soil, on high or low land, there is in Britain such an array of trees, shrubs and plants gathered from every temperate country of the world that we never need despair of filling any site adequately. And it must be admitted that, though there is today a marked and reviving interest in the history of garden design and all that pertains to it, English people are mainly interested in plants, more and more plants, and many of them. This is of course what makes our gardens so interesting to all plant lovers, most of whom are themselves trying to create beautiful gardens.

Joining the Garden to the House

In order to succeed, a garden has to be well suited to the house it surrounds. Most of us like to sit in our gardens when conditions are right, and as a rule our sitting places are within easy reach of the house. It is all bound up with the storage of chairs, the carrying of trays, and the cosiness of sitting with our backs to a wall or dense hedge. In addition, our sitting places are usually paved. The transition is from the rooms of the house to the areas – or "rooms" – of the garden. Formality walks out of the house in all well-designed gardens: the movement is from the strictly formal house-rooms to the rooms of the garden which are less formal in detail, though they may not be so in design. Immediately we leave the house the plants to some extent take over; they may be prim beds of roses, or even bedding plants on a terrace, but in today's garden sooner or later they give way to shrubs. Scarcely any shrubs can be considered formal unless they are clipped or pruned into compact masses or hedges. This change from flowers to shrubs is the first step in the transition. Far be it from me to claim that this gradual movement is the only recipe for successful garden design, but it is at least traditional. Even so, today's predilection for being different results in some totally opposed informal designs, successful to many eyes.

On entering the garden from the house we usually feel a need to allow some of the luxury and colour to spread outside. This is perhaps where the greatest gathering of colour can be enjoyed and encouraged; everyone loves to see plenty of flowers from the windows. The colour will not only come from flowers, because so much can be done to bolster their effect – which in many plants quickly passes – by the use of foliage other than green. There

The contrast of the rounded head of Stone Pines, left, and slender Mediterranean Cypresses was the inspiration of many artists in the eighteenth century. This sort of contrast of shapes can be repeated with many other trees and shrubs, in landscapes or gardens of any size. Photographed in the South of France.

will also be the differing textures of paving or gravel, lawn and flower beds or borders, severe hedges and perhaps a pool. The planting, too, can accentuate the variety of shapes by the use once again of the contrast between the vertical and the rounded, as would be obtained with the Lombardy Poplar and the Lebanon Cedar. I am not suggesting that either of these trees can be accommodated in a modern suburban garden but the same dramatic contrast can be repeated down the scale with various pairs of plants: a columnar cypress with *Viburnum plicatum* 'Mariesii' perhaps, or a fastigiate *Koelreuteria* with a flat juniper, or the spiky leaves of a *Phormium* against a grey hummock of lavender. Yet smaller, for the tiniest gardens, we could use the slow *Juniperus communis* 'Compressa' against a carpet of crisp leaves of London Pride. There are endless possibilities in this one simple scheme alone; the student could hardly be better occupied than in seeking out combinations with this kind of contrast in various sizes and qualities, for varying conditions.

This is but one idea in what is an ever-extending galaxy of plants with every possible diversity with which we can experiment. Just as we saw in earlier chapters the range of leaf and greenery from which we could choose to enliven our landscape, so in the garden with its vastly richer ingredients we can play the dark green against the grey, the coppery tint against the yellowish or glaucous, the glittering leaves against the matt, the large against the small. Once again it is useful and advantageous to use the large leaves near at hand; the broad blades of *Bergenia* and *Hosta* will act in the same way as the wild Burdock in the natural landscape, to increase the perspective. In addition to mere size and surface, there is the narrow leaf of grasses and irises to contrast with the broad of *Rodgersia*; the tiny leaves of heathers and conifers to give a dense receding appearance while the silvery greys appear to come forward.

Apart from all this we have variegation of foliage which is so much to the fore in gardeners' thoughts these days. Here we are on dangerous ground. In our thirst for colours other than green we are apt to use variegation to excess. The bizarre - for that is what variegation amounts to - can be easily overdone, and its dramatic light reduced to the commonplace, if it is not used circumspectly, to accentuate a point of design or lighten a statement in greens. Each variegated plant should have a great bearing upon the choice of its neighbours, and should act as a complement to the temporary flowering of another plant and be there to take its place before and after its flowering.

Contrast is not everything, however. It is almost inevitable in today's gardens where many diverse plants are grown. Its thoughtful use adds much to the garden, but in some areas it is better to revert to the Jekyll idea of variation within the theme rather than the upsetting effect of constant contrast. Green is so beautiful that when used entirely on its own it can bring one up short with the thought, "Why haven't I done that before?" There are similar successful schemes using other colours in such gardens as Hidcote, Sissinghurst, Tintinhull. The plan may be that easiest of specialities the white garden or border, or a combination of, say, two colours. The sharp tones can be augmented with yellowish foliage, the soft tones - the pinks, magentas and mauves - with grey foliage. The coppery-toned foliage will assort with both, fortunately, making it specially valuable in uniting a pair of borders of disparate colours. I have written at length about this fascinating study in my *Perennial Garden Plants*. There is never a last word on the matter and we all have different ideals.

On coming out of the house, therefore, we may expect to meet a contrived planting where every artifice can be used to make the immediate garden appear to have spilled out of the building. We should find the colours – linking perhaps to those in the rooms – and the contrasts or gentle variations within the theme, the firm lines of paths and hedges, and the seats to tempt us to linger.

Transition from Garden to Landscape

When we rise from the garden seat and make our way farther from the house we begin the transition from garden to landscape. After the richness near at hand we need new sensations, not more of the same kind. The eye should not be continually excited any more than the palate, or all will pall with surfeit. From the richness at hand we can progress towards more sober planting, where hard lines are eschewed and vivid colours are left behind. In any really carefully arranged planting there is one point in the transition

Dudmaston, Shropshire, a National Trust property. A successful blending of garden into landscape.

where the eye says, "Thus far and no farther; beyond is landscape, not garden." Having left behind all the garish non-green leaves we can concentrate merely upon the greens, the dark or light; the glossy, the matt; the large, the small. The worst thing to do is to plant a yellow acacia (*Robinia*) or variegated *Elaeagnus* to accentuate the distance. In reality it has the opposite effect: by reducing the perspective it foreshortens the distance. A scarlet azalea or a white flower can do the same, whereas if the flowers are of soft tones of pink, yellow, blue or mauve, all is well. As a rule the cooler colours are best in the distance and the same applies to foliage tints. They suggest the soft focus of distance, even if they are only a few yards away. By adopting this colour sequence and supplementing it by using bold foliage near at hand and grading down to tiny foliage farther away, a surprising effect of distance can be gained in quite a small plot.

In the larger gardens, where the backcloth is the countryside, the same of course applies. We have to decide where the garden ends and the landscape starts. Usually this will be marked by a boundary of some kind, but, as Repton pointed out, a hard line across the view should be avoided. The ideal is a ha-ha or sunken fence; if, however, a hard line of some kind seems inevitable, it should be disguised by informal planting – on *both* sides if possible.

One of the hardest lines in the great gardens of the National Trust is at Polesden Lacey, Surrey, where the transition from sloping lawn to the splendid prospect of parkland and Ranmore is severed by the oblique line of yew hedge. The crowning insult to the eye was a series of squares of clipped hedge above the general line – like well-spaced castellations – but these were removed some years ago. It was senseless to continue clipping such excrescences, even though they were part of the history of the place. There is a ha-ha but it is not deep enough to exclude cattle, hence the hedge above it. One day, perhaps, we shall be able to afford to remake it. At Trelissick, Cornwall, the construction of a ha-ha has resulted in some superlative views of the parkland and estuary. I have been tempted more than once to claim it to be the most beautiful of all views from the Trust's gardens. These two examples serve as extremes in presenting the prospect from a garden, where there is a definite line of transition.

Two of the most delightful transitions – successful because they are almost imperceptible – are at Rowallane, Co. Down, where the garden planting seems to echo the local scenery with trees and hillocks, and at Antony House in Devon. Here the terraces meet sloping lawns and the land falls away to the distant prospect, much as Repton designed it all those years ago. At Florence Court, Co. Fermanagh, on the garden front with its great weeping beeches, and at Ascott, Buckinghamshire, the transitions are equally gentle.

There is often this gentle division in our great gardens. The lie of the land

and the River Thames do it for us at renowned Cliveden; a ha-ha on the south side of the house at Bodnant, North Wales, divides the garden from the native oaks on the little knoll in the meadow. A lake separates the two elements in a wholly satisfying way at Dudmaston. At Clevedon Court, Avon, a fence sunk below the lawn does not interrupt the view across the meadows to the distant houses and church tower, while so vast is the landscape at Powis Castle it is no easy matter for the newcomer to decide at what point the garden ends.

The lessons learnt at Hidcote are that, as a rule, vistas should end without a full stop. The great gates invite us onwards to views over the countryside; the big vine-leaves act in the same way that Burdock does in the landscape, enhancing the perspective of the dim distant view. The planting of the stream banks goes from strong colours to white, easily enticing the eye over the meadows, and the point of transition is not made obvious by the ha-ha. Francis Bacon in his essay *On Gardening* made the point that no hedges should hinder our view of the prospect beyond.

Perhaps the most remarkable of transitions from garden to landscape is found at Blickling Hall, Norfolk. If we look out from the east side of the house, there is a flat garden parterre ending in broad steps from which a long gravel walk extends up rising lawns to a distant temple, flanked by what look like belts of eighteenth-century trees grouped informally alongside. These trees are in reality the outcome of a formal "wilderness" of 1729. We do not look out upon the countryside until we are beyond the temple, when the direction of the vista is extended by a double avenue of chestnuts and beeches. An old estate map shows the main formal lines on the other side of the house. These have long disappeared, while the east side and, indeed, the north side with its half mile-long lake have been developed during the last two hundred years or so.

Just where the actual point of transition is reached is a matter of taste, expedience or necessity. For over a hundred years we gardeners have been inclined to extend our gardens into the landscape by planting exotic trees in rough grass. This tendency has been caused by the ever-present desire to augment our collections and at the same time to avoid saddling ourselves with any kind of planting which may increase our liability in labour and attention. It started in the early nineteenth century with arboreta, containing all the new great conifers, and it continues today with *Nothofagus*, *Magnolia* and *Sorbus*. This last genus, composed of small to medium-sized trees, lends itself particularly well to the restricted resources of garden owners today. It may please some to decorate the landscape with such lesser trees, but so doing will negate all that Repton and Jekyll have taught us.

9

SOME PARKS AND LANDSCAPES IN THE NATIONAL TRUST

The following list has been selected from the National Trust's List of Properties. The properties comprise substantial areas of countryside in which landscape qualities of all sorts constitute an important element.

Note: The inclusion of a property in this list does not necessarily mean that it is open to members and the public; reference should be made to the Trust's literature for guidance on this matter.

ENGLAND

Avon
Dyrham Park. 274 acres. Parkland around the house (including the site of the late-seventeenth-century water garden by George London). Mediaeval in origin, it was landscaped by Charles Harcourt Masters in 1798. After the destruction of elms by disease extensive replanting has been done (late 1970s). The fallow deer herd is one of the oldest in the country.
Failand. 363 acres. Farmland interspersed with small woods. From the crests of the higher parts are views over the Avon and the Bristol Channel, to Bristol 6 miles north.
Rainbow Wood. 243 acres. On the outskirts of Bath; farmland and woods above the valley.

Berkshire
Basildon Park. 406 acres. Park and woodland possibly landscaped by Capability Brown, to whom small sums were paid in 1778.
Maidenhead Thicket and Manor of Cookham. 843 acres. Mainly common and manorial waste with pastures, woods, thickets of thorn and underwood and some arable land.

Buckinghamshire
Bradenham. 1,111 acres. Village and farmlands across a dry valley of the Chilterns sweeping up to exceptionally fine beech woods on the hills above.
Cliveden. 439 acres. Mostly woodlands above the Thames, with formal rides

laid out c. 1720, possibly by Charles Bridgeman.

Hughenden. 169 acres. Woods and meadows surrounding the house and church with a chalk stream through the small park.

Waddesdon. 160 acres. A rounded hill, rising from the vale of Aylesbury emparked and planted with semi-mature trees at the time the house was built (1874–89). There is a herd of Sika deer and free-flying macaws.

West Wycombe Park. 300 acres. The park contains lakes, a stream and eighteenth-century lodges, temples and cascade. The landscape was laid out in two stages; c. 1740, in semi-formal style, and between 1770 and 1775, when Nicholas Revett and Humphry Repton worked in the park.

Cambridgeshire

Wicken Fen. 730 acres. Mere, dykes, reed and sedge fen; alder buckthorn and willow carr with some pastures.

Wimpole Hall. 2,443 acres. Bridgeman, Greening, Brown and Repton all worked in the park (1,000 acres). Bridgeman's grand double elm avenue is in course of replanting with lime after destruction by disease. The Castle Folly is by Sanderson Miller and lies beyond the lake and stream which is spanned by a "Chinese" bridge. Beyond the circuit planting is heavy clay arable farmland.

Cheshire

Lyme Park. 1,321 acres. Emparked in the fourteenth century, and has a long established fallow deer herd. Wooded cloughs and grass pastures around the house rise to high heather moorland. Ancient short avenue of Common Lime, Elizabethan tower, "The Cage"; Lanthorn Tower built of stone from the lantern of the original house.

Styal. 252 acres. Farm and woodlands "derelaged" to serve the great water-powered cotton mill (1784). The power came from the River Bollin which runs through a steep-sided wooded valley.

Tatton Park. 2,086 acres. The park was planned by Humphry Repton, and includes Tatton Mere, and an avenue of limes. Herd of fallow deer.

Cornwall

Cotehele. 1,287 acres. Farm and woodlands above the tidal Tamar. Small steep fields were formerly devoted to early flower and vegetable crops for the London market. Hanging woods above the river and up the Morden Valley. A water mill of mediaeval origin, estate workshops, quay and sailing barge.

Helford River. 362 acres. Mainly woodland, including Mawnan Glebe, planted with Holm Oak in the year of Trafalgar, Tremayne Woods, and natural oak woodland reaching down to the water's edge.

Lanhydrock. 900 acres. The avenue approaching the house was planted with

Sycamores in 1648 and both this avenue and its duplicate rows (planted in 1790) have since been patched with beech.

Penrose. 1,536 acres. Farms and wooded valleys running down to the Loe, a freshwater lake a mile long held from the sea by a shingle bar. Carminowe Creek forms an arm of the lake.

St Anthony in Roseland. 470 acres. A high peninsula between the sea, on which side it is windswept farmland, and the St Mawes estuary, sheltered and wooded for a mile and continuing so up the west side of Froe Creek.

Trelissick. 376 acres. Park and farmland with woods dipping down to the River Fal at King Harry ferry and spreading south to form a salient into the estuary. Tree belts form an almost continuous edging on the seaward side.

Cumbria

Borrowdale and Derwentwater. 5,342 acres. Lake and islands, woods, farms, parkland and fell. Includes the natural oak of Great Wood, the Manesty Park larch and the pine wood, and the promontory of Friar's Crag.

Coniston Water and Monk Coniston. 4,821 acres. Farmland with trees scattered and in clumps, and woodland all by the lakeside, and rising to moor and woodland towards Little Langdale and around the pine-clad islands of the man-made Tarn Hows.

Glencoyne Park and Gowbarrow Parks. 3,446 acres. Farmland and fell with natural oak woods above and below the cataract and waterfalls of Aira Force, all on the north shore of Ullswater.

Langdales. 2,355 acres. Farms, small woods running up to the heads of the dales.

Nether Wasdale. 1,490 acres. Farmland with belts of trees and woods astride the River Irt.

Sizergh Castle. 1,562 acres. Farmland and woods round the house (pele tower 1340) including oak and hazel coppice, descending to moss on the east and rising to a high ridge of rough pasture to the south.

Windermere. 1,424 acres. On the west of the lake the Claife woodlands, Wray Castle and farmland and woods at High and Low Wray.

Derbyshire

Dovedale. 1,100 acres. Woodland and pastures along 6 miles of the river to the gorge. There are limestone rock features, caves and arches and an extensive range of ecological succession from pasture to climax woodland.

Hardwick Hall. 2,305 acres. Farmland with small woods and park where there are vestiges of ancient forest. The main approach is a clump-planted (nineteenth century) oak avenue, and a double row of limes in a half-circle to the east of the house (c. 1930). Recent replanting in the park and new plantings on restored open-cast mine sites in the farmland. Tudor fishponds and eighteenth-century lakes with duck decoy.

Hope Woodlands and Edale. 18,313 acres. High moorland with farmland in Edale and on the Snake road (nearly 2,000 acres in all) with small woodlands in the dales and especially along the rivers Noe and Ashop.

Longshaw. 1,486 acres. Moor, wood and farmland on the Gritstone Edge, including the Barbage Brook which runs through the relict Sessile Oak woods of Padley Gorge. Iron Age field systems survive, also abandoned grinding-stone quarries.

Devon

Arlington Court. 3,000 acres. Park, woods and farmland. The River Yeo feeds a lake and runs through 2 miles of deep and wooded valley. Notable European Silver Fir and *Araucaria*. Shetland pony herd, Jacob's sheep and wild red deer. The farm structure and fields are of Celtic origin.

Branscombe & Weston. 500 acres. Farmland in valleys running down to the sea and on the cliff tops, with small woods on the steeper scarps and landslip undercliff.

Hembury, Holne and Bridford Woods. 762 acres. In the valleys of the Dart and the Teign a complex of semi-natural woodland, plantations and coppice oak. Wild daffodils by the rivers. A hilltop Iron Age fort at Hembury.

Killerton. 6,388 acres. Park, woods and farmland, with village and hamlets, lying across the valleys of the Clyst and Culm. The woods have a wide spectrum of species including nineteenth-century conifer introductions. The farmlands are planted with hedgerow trees and small woods.

North Devon Coast. 3,350 acres. Farm and woodland, cliff and moor including the deep valley of the Lyn above and below Watersmeet and the natural oakwoods there and at Heddon's Mouth.

Saltram. 468 acres. Parkland, mostly farmed.

South Hams. 2,114 acres. Along the coast from Prawle to Hope, and separately on the Yealm (555 acres). Farmland and cliff grazing with woods in sheltered places. Includes the Nine Mile carriage drive (nineteenth century) around The Warren, Noss Mayo.

Dorset

Brownsea Island. 500 acres. Heath and woodland, with relict traces of farm and bulb fields, and of clay and pyrites mining. Freshwater lakes and lagoon. Maritime and Scots Pine naturally regenerated after the fire of 1933.

Golden Cap. 1,970 acres. Farmland and rough grazings, cliff and undercliff, small woods and bog. The landscape pattern is complex and agriculture is controlled to maintain this and promote conservation.

East Sussex

Bateman's. 300 acres. Farmland along the valley below Burwash. The hedgerows and the trees in them are the essence of the character of this enclosed landscape.

Crowlink. 690 acres. Chalk downland farmed within the guidelines of a management plan in arable and permanent pasture, with areas of natural gorse and thorn thickets all sweeping down to open grassland above high chalk cliffs.

Wickham Manor Farm, Winchelsea. 392 acres. Farmland, mainly pasture including much of the site of the original "Ancient Town", a post windmill, the steep and wooded scarp above the marsh and 1½ miles of the Royal Military Canal.

Essex

Danbury. 297 acres. Common land with dense thickets of thorn and gorse, birch woods and the chestnut coppice (83 acres) of Blake's Wood.

Hatfield Forest. 1,049 acres. Ancient royal forest; rolling, timbered country. Lake, 1746. Shell House (folly) c. 1757.

Gloucestershire

The Cotswold Edge. 2,080 acres. Four separate but similar areas of pasture, rough grazing and woodland characteristic of the steep escarpment.

Greater Manchester

Dunham Massey. 3,204 acres, mostly farmed. Formal park with radiating avenues, laid out in the early eighteenth century. Park contains an obelisk, deer barn, slaughterhouse and seventeenth-century water mill. Herd of fallow deer.

Hampshire

Bramshaw Commons. 1,392 acres. Typical New Forest commons set off by areas of heath and plantations. Ponds and wetlands.

Ludshott Commons. 932 acres. Mainly heathland on sandstone ridge, pine woods recently damaged by fire. A string of hammer ponds at Waggoners' Wells in a wooded valley. Passfield and Conford Commons comprise damp grass commons with some woodland.

Mottisfont Abbey. 1,645 acres, mostly farmed, with a woodland pattern. A tributary of the River Test runs through the grounds. Rustic fishing hut.

Hereford and Worcester

Berrington Hall. 455 acres of farm and parkland including 75 acres woodland; landscaped by Capability Brown in 1780, including the Pool.

Brockhampton. 1,650 acres. Farmland and woods. There are exceptionally fine Sessile Oak of a great age, and magnificent ash grow in the dingles. The hedgerows retain many old damson trees and mistletoe grows on the orchard and hedgerow trees. A modest park and small lake in the woods.

Croft Castle. 1,385 acres. Mainly park, wood and common land. Avenues of oak and Spanish Chestnut. Fish Pool Valley laid out in late eighteenth century in the Picturesque style. Mistletoe grows on the oak trees around the Iron Age hill fort of Croft Ambrey.

Hertfordshire

Ashridge Estate. 3,944 acres. Common, woods and farmland on the crest of the Chilterns, running out to the promontory of Ivinghoe Beacon. Ancient wood-grazing pollard beech survive at Frithsden, and there are numerous examples of very old oak, beech and Spanish Chestnut. A collection of hardwood species was begun in 1980 and is in progress.

Isle of Wight

Newton. 223 acres with 14 miles of river estuary and 4 miles of Solent foreshore. The site of the settlement founded in 1256 by the Bishop of Winchester of which the burgage plots and road network survive as hedgerows and green lanes, with a very few habitations remaining. The elm hedgerow trees have been destroyed by disease and are replaced by new plantings of other species. Quay, saltpans and oyster fishing.

South Wight. 806 acres. From St Catherine's Point eastward through St Boniface Down to the great landslip area of Luccombe; a complex of pasture, downland grazings, wood, cliff and undercliff. Above Ventnor on the face of the down, of exceeding steepness, is a thicket of Holm Oak grown from acorns set in the early twentieth century.

West Wight. 1,997 acres, seven miles along the coast from the Needles to Mottistone. Farmland, chalk down, heath and rough grazings, with small woods in sheltered spots, with both chalk cliff and lias clay.

Kent

Scotney Castle. 782 acres. Farm and woodland with hop fields and oasts. Picturesque moated ruin, realised by Sawrey Gilpin c. 1850.

Westerham. 421 acres. Beech, oak and coppice woodlands of Toys and Ide Hills, Wealden woods and farmland of Crockham Hill with oasts at Outridge.

Lincolnshire

Gunby Hall. 1,400 acres. Farm, wood and park at the southern tip of the Wolds. There is a record of tree planting in the park since 1665, and there are clearly recognisable remains of the formal layout. The farmlands are interspersed with small woods and tree belts, and the hedgerow planting has recently been renewed. Remains of the moated site of Bratoft Manor and of the deserted village of Gunby.

London

Osterley Park. 140 acres. Park and lakes from the seventeenth century; temple c. 1720; garden house 1780; ice house. The outline of the early planting can be discerned and is being restored.

River Wandle. 140 acres. Morden Park and Watermeads bestride the river. There is a wide range of tree species and some very large White Willows. Herons fish the waters.

Norfolk

Blickling Hall. 4,767 acres. Farms, woods and parkland. The park, of mediaeval origin, was taken for farming in 1939 and is now in the process of restoration. Hedges date from Tudor enclosure. The half mile-long lake dates from before 1770.

Felbrigg Hall. 1,800 acres, mostly farmed. Woodland and lakeside walks. Some fine trees remain from the seventeenth century. Ice house.

Horsey Estate. 1,734 acres. Horsey Mere (120 acres), reed and sedge fen surrounded by farmland and running out to Marram dunes at Horsey Gap.

North Norfolk Coast. 6,014 acres. Marsh, saltings and dunes, sand and shingle spits and beaches. Includes Blakeney Point, Scolt Island, Brancaster and Stiffkey Marshes.

Northumberland

Bellister. 1,122 acres. Farmland and moor, with woods on the scarp of the valley of the South Tyne.

Cragside. 940 acres. A tributary of the River Coquet is dammed to form Tumbleton lake and then descends through a narrow valley in which grow magnificent North American conifers. Woods rise very steeply from the river to a high whinstone ridge where there are three more lakes. Among the pine woods there are tracts of *Rhododendron ponticum* and *Gaultheria shallon,* and wide flat tables of bare whinstone. Many pathways and a circuit drive: all designed and planted in the late nineteenth century.

Embleton Links. 520 acres. From the fishing village of Low Newton (inclusive) south to Dunstanburgh Castle (also inclusive), the dune complex ending in the low basalt outcrop of the castle site.

Hadrian's Wall. 1,896 acres. Permanent pasture and rough grazing astride 4 miles of the wall, down to and across the Military Road. Small woods of Sycamore and pine grow on the whinstone crags and in sheltered places.

Wallington. 12,970 acres. Farmland rising to moors, with parkland, ponds and woods near the house, dating from the eighteenth century. The Lake at Rothley was by Brown (who was born in the next parish) and the Wansbeck Bridge by Paine.

North Yorkshire

Bridestones and Crosscliffe. 1,205 acres. Farmland, woods and moor with an exposure of eroded rocks. There are barrows and earthworks.

Ravenscar. 444 acres. In several parcels from the northern tip of Robin Hood's Bay along four miles of the coast southward. Farmland, disused alum workings, woods and thickets, cliff and landslip undercliff and the hanging waterfall of Hayburn Wyke.

Nottinghamshire
Clumber Park. 3,784 acres, approximately 700 acres of which are farmed. The eighteenth-century layout is likely to have been by Stephen Wright, pupil of William Kent, who also designed the house, some of the lodges, the two temples and the Classical bridge over the upper lake. Designs were continued by R. White of Retford (also a pupil of Kent) after Wright's death. Lincoln Terrace by William Sawrey Gilpin. The lakes are fed by the River Poulter.

Oxfordshire
Buscot and Coleshill. 7,843 acres. Farm and woodland with small park and two lakes. Water meadows by the Thames. The former elm tree landscape was destroyed by disease and is now being restored with other species.
Whitehorse Hill. 235 acres. Mainly downland, much of it recently restored from arable, around Uffington Castle, the Horse and its Manger, and the Dragon Hill.

Shropshire
Attingham Park. 3,826 acres. Mainly arable farmland with woods and pastures along the Tern and Severn rivers; the ancient park was later worked by Thomas Legett in 1770 and landscaped by Repton in 1797. There is a herd of fallow deer, enclosed by a fence of riven oak. The site of Roman Uriconium lies below the south-west corner of the estate.
Dudmaston. 2,320 acres. Woodland, farms and a park, for which William Emes was consulted on a design for 70 acres in 1777. Major landscaping dates from the 1850s when the Big Pool was made. The Dingle, which runs down to the Severn, was landscaped on the model of Shenstone's *ferme ornée*, The Leasowes, and is being restored. It contains fine Small-leafed Lime of great age. During the period 1920-40 derelict farms on light land were planted to form new woods of pine, larch and hardwoods.
Long Mynd. 4,530 acres. Mainly common land with grass, heather pastures and gorse thickets with trees growing in sheltered sites forming a self-contained massif facing Wales. 14 barrows, 3 linear entrenchments and $3\frac{1}{2}$ miles of the Port Way.
Wilderhope Manor. 237 acres. Farmland round the little-altered Tudor house, looking down Corvedale and across to the hanging oakwood on the far scarp.

Somerset
Holnicote. 12,434 acres. From the shore of the Bristol Channel over the hills of Bossington and Selworthy down across the Porlock Vale and up and over Dunkery Beacon, a complex of farmland, woods and moor. Included

are the villages of Allerford, Bossington, Luccombe and Selworthy. The woods are of great variety – Holm Oak by Bossington, Douglas Fir on the slope below Exmoor, natural Scots Pine at Webber's Post and natural or coppice oak (800 acres) in Horner. The hedgerows of the vale are being restocked with trees. Two pack horse bridges, groups of barrows, a stone circle and Iron Age fort.

Montacute. 303 acres. The wide avenue to the east was the original approach. Park and some farmland. Look-out tower on St Michael's Hill.

South Yorkshire

Derwent Estate. 5,077 acres. The east side of Derwent dale head, pasture fields with tree groups in places rising to high grass and heather moor.

Staffordshire

Hawksmoor. 307 acres. Wood, heath and farmland in the Churnet valley.

Kinver Edge. 285 acres. High heath and woodland, which run out to an Iron Age promontory fort above mediaeval rock dwellings.

Manifold and Hamps Valleys. 598 acres. Woods and grazing lands in these limestone valleys where the rivers intermittently run below ground, from Beeston Tor (the cliff and cove), to Ilam Hall where both rivers re-emerge. Hinkley Wood contains ancient Small-Leaf Lime and superabundant Hart's Tongue fern. In Ilam Park the raised plots and furrows of the village's mediaeval open field system survive intact.

Shugborough. 952 acres. Parkland, in which there are notable neo-Grecian ornamental buildings, and woodland. The home farm houses a herd of Longhorn cattle and other rare breeds.

Suffolk

Dunwich Heath. 214 acres. Heathland along a mile of sandy cliffs. Erosion by the sea has engulfed the town.

Ickworth. 1,792 acres. The park (600 acres) was formed from ancient woodland. (Brown is thought to have worked here.) The rest is half woodland, half farm. Oak of exceptional quality grows in the woods, and cedar, Holm Oak and Redwoods of great size in those near the house. There is a thatched summer house, obelisk, church, and a small lake by the kitchen garden.

Surrey

Box Hill, Mickleham and Headley Heath. 1,534 acres. Along the east scarp of the Mole where it flows through the Mickleham Gap in the North Downs, a complex of downland, with natural vegetation of yew, box, juniper, thorn and beech, with mixed woods, farmland and some chalk heath. The natural history of the area has been recorded in detail over a long period.

Frensham Common. 969 acres. Heath with some pine woods, the Great and Little Ponds and marsh.

Harewoods and Sand Hills. 2,478 acres. Farmland with small woods and the common of Outwood, it lies at the foot of the North Downs running from the greensand ridge on to heavy clay and exemplifies the pattern of Wealden enclosure.

Hatchlands. 400 acres. Farm and woodland. Eighteenth-century ice house. Original drive from old Portsmouth-London road was superseded by new drive and lodges from West Horsley village in the early twentieth century, by H. S. Goodhart Rendel. It is probable that Benjamin Armitage in 1767 and, later, Humphry Repton advised on the parkland.

Hindhead. 1,400 acres. The high greensand ridge includes Gibbet Hill and the Devil's Punchbowl. Pine and heath, formerly worked for broom-making by gipsy-like "broom squires".

Polesden Lacey and Ranmore. 1,830 acres. On the syncline of the North Downs, farmland with belts of trees and larger woods reaching east through the wooded common of Ranmore to the chalk scarp of the Mickleham Gap with natural downland flora.

Witley and Milford Commons. 377 acres. Common land with wide variety of woodland and open habitats with resulting rich natural history interest. Wetland areas. National Trust Information Centre.

Warwickshire

Charlecote Park. 278 acres. Park and farm. Capability Brown was forbidden to fell the ancient avenue of Common Limes, but altered the line of the River Avon, and remodelled a portion of the park, creating the North Garden. Fallow and red deer.

Farnborough Hall. 389 acres. Farmland encloses famous Landscape Garden of the late eighteenth century, laid out by William Holbech, assisted by Sanderson Miller, containing great grass terrace and an intricate design of connected lakes. Two eighteenth-century temples and obelisk.

West Sussex

Blackdown and Marley. 772 acres. Heathland recently heavily colonised by naturally seeded Scots Pine with beech hangers. Ancient trackway, Penny-bush (Pen-y-bos) Lane to the "Temple of the Winds" high above the Weald. Hammer Ponds at Shottermill.

Drovers. 1,058 acres. Arable farmland interspersed with woods of beech and oak, hazel coppice with standards and some conifers. It lies within the folds of the South Downs. A lavant breaks above Cucumbers' Farm to flow through Singleton.

Nymans. 601 acres. Farmland and woods around the house and garden and the small park. Deep gills with outcrops of greensand rock run down to a stream and lake through woods in which grow oak, ash and North American conifers.

Petworth House. 738 acres. One of Capability Brown's masterpieces complete with lake and majestic trees. Traces of earlier formal garden design west of the house remain from Elizabethan design, and by George London c. 1690. Temples by Brown in Pleasure Grounds north of the house.

Slindon. 3,500 acres. A 6-mile long cross-section of the South Downs from the north-facing scarp with beech hangers, over high downland, overlying the clay with flint covering of the southern syncline and on over the clays and gravels beyond. Farmland is intermixed with woods of oak and beech, larch and pine. Park Wood contains beech of exceptional height, girth and fine form. There are Iron Age barrows, cross-ridge dykes and a village with its field system, and the Roman Stane Street (AD 70) runs terraced up the scarp and then embanked and ditched, for 3½ miles.

Woolbeding. 1,102 acres. Farmland, woods and commons (400 acres) on the lower greensand of the Weald astride the River Rother.

West Yorkshire

Hebden Dale. 402 acres. Mainly woodland planted in the mid-nineteenth century by the 1st Baron Savil to landscape the approach to his shooting moors.

Wiltshire

Avebury. 910 acres. Arable farmland surrounding the unique Megalithic monument and other Neolithic remains, and the mediaeval village.

Lacock Abbey. 320 acres. Farmland round the village with park running down to water meadows by the Avon, which is spanned by a stone bridge.

Stonehenge Down. 1,500 acres. Formerly open down but since 1940 fenced arable farmland with a few small woods. Very numerous Neolithic and Bronze Age monuments, the Avenue and the Cursus.

Stourhead. 2,507 acres. Mainly farmland and woods around the house and pleasure grounds from which the landscaping extends as a terrace leading past an obelisk, round the head of the valley of St Peter's Pump, and up to the brick-built Alfred's Tower overlooking the Somerset vale.

WALES

Clwyd

Chirk Castle. 481 acres. Parkland, now farmed, planted by William Emes from 1764, and woods above the River Ceiriog. Wrought iron entrance gates by the Davies Brothers, 1719.

Erddig. 1,138 acres. Park, farm and woodland round the house (which retains its domestic offices and workshops). A museum of agricultural equipment at Felin Puleston with working horses. There is an ornamental hydraulic system including the "Cup and Saucer". Some 460 acres of parkland planted by William Emes from 1764, and partly in Victorian times. Remnants of formal seventeenth-century planting also survive.

Dyfed

Colby. 870 acres. Steep-sided narrow wooded valleys converging and running towards the sea, surrounded by well hedged farmland with trees.

Dolaucothi. 2,577 acres. Farm and woodland, including extensive oak coppices in the Cothi valley. A gold mine, where some workings and an aqueduct remain from Roman times, was still worked in the early twentieth century.

Pembrokeshire Coast. 1,932 acres. Farmland with small woods in sheltered cwms leading to the sea among the cliffs, promontories and coves.

Stackpole. 1,992 acres. 8 miles of coast with cliffs, dune systems and deep coves, backed by farmlands and small woods. The eighteenth-century policy woods of the former Court and freshwater lakes still remain.

Gwent

Clytha Park and Coed-y-Bwynydd. 396 acres. Park and farmland rising to an Iron Age hill fort near which is a Gothick castle folly.

Sugar Loaf. 2,130 acres. Common lands of grass, heather and bracken, with small woods, the high point (600 m or 1,955 ft) of which looks out over the vale of Usk.

Gwynedd

Dolmelynllyn. 1,249 acres. Upland estate, planted in eighteenth and early nineteenth centuries in the Picturesque style.

Lleyn Peninsula. 2,000 acres. Coast and farmland including the Plas-yn-Rhiw estate (416 acres).

Penrhyn Castle, Carneddau and Yspytty. 41,727 acres. Mountain and moorland, farms and woodland with the rivers Llugwy, Machno and Conwy. Extensive recent tree planting in the Yspytty farmlands.

Powys

Brecon Beacons. 9,000 acres. Mainly the central massif of high open moor with partly wooded valley heads and the farmland of Blaenglyn.

West Glamorgan

The Gower. 4,578 acres. Salt marsh, beach, dune, down, cliff and woodland all round the peninsula. Much is common land.

NORTHERN IRELAND

Co. Antrim

North Antrim Coast. 1,500 acres. Cliff, dune and beach with pastures and woods above, much of it linked with the Trust's 10-mile coastal path to

White Park Bay. The Giant's Causeway, Dunseverick Castle, the rope bridge of Carrick-a-Rede and the village of Cushendun are included. The great amphitheatre of Murlough Bay with its woods, pastures and streams falling to the beach is of exceptional beauty.

Co. Armagh

Ardress House. 100 acres. Farm and parkland round the house and garden with a circuit walk through the tree belt of the park. There is a museum of farm equipment.

The Argory. 292 acres. Woods and pasture around the house and along the River Blackwater. There are walks, including the Lime Walk, which use cottages on the property as their focal points.

Co. Down

Castle Ward. 792 acres. Demesne lands of the castle comprising farm and woodland running down to a mile length of the south shore of Strangford Lough. A great formal water garden (seventeenth century) with a raised terrace beyond and temple (eighteenth century) focuses on Audley's Tower (fifteenth century) by the lough side.

Lisnabreeny. 156 acres. On the edge of Belfast; from a deep glen with a waterfall, farmland and woods run up to a high knoll of rough pasture.

Minnowburn Beeches. 128 acres. $3\frac{1}{2}$ miles from central Belfast woods and pastures by the River Lagan.

Mount Stewart. 418 acres. Woods and fields round the house and grounds run along the north side of the head of Strangford Lough to the "Temple of the Winds" (c. 1780) on a hillock above the lough.

Murlough, Dundrum. 938 acres. Extensive dune systems partly stabilised and forming woodland.

Co. Fermanagh

Castlecoole. 78 acres. Parkland planted c. 1750 by W. King and in the nineteenth century by J. Frazer to form the whole setting for this great house.

Co. Londonderry

Springhill. 60 acres. Pastures surrounding the house from which the Beech Walk (replanted 1981) leads to the Mill Tower. A yew grove survives from the seventeenth century.

10

TREES THROUGH OTHER EYES AND MINDS

No cedar broad
Drops his dark curtain where a distant scene
Demands distinction. Here the thin abele
Of lofty bole, and bare, the smooth-stem'd beech,
Or slender alder, give to our eye free space
Beneath their boughs to catch each lessening charm
Ev'n to the far horizon's azure bound.

William Mason (1728-97)

In the earlier sections of this book I have tried to show first what might be achieved and then the ingredients available. I have been at pains to stress that the first approach in every instance should be from the viewpoint of aesthetics adjusted as necessary by practical contingencies, as was the case in the eighteenth century. At that time whole schemes were instigated by artists and poets; the landscape and its trees were their preoccupation and their ideas transformed much of our countryside. I therefore feel we owe it to them, in conclusion, to devote a few pages to examining the ways in which trees have appealed to artists and poets.

The shapes of trees have fascinated painters for centuries. A common example in Italian and French paintings was the contrast between the thin spires of the Mediterranean Cypress and the rounded head of the Stone Pine, a dramatic effect learnt subconsciously by all planters. In the colder climate of Britain it is repeated in countless landscapes and gardens by the use of the Lombardy Poplar and one of our rounded deciduous trees, or, in even stronger contrast, a Lebanon Cedar. In gardens the space problem is solved by the use of one of the smaller American conifers and a shrub of rounded outline. One of the best pictures showing Lombardy Poplars is by Alfred Parsons, who excelled in painting flowers and garden views; it is entitled "Poplars in the Thames Valley".

The vertical line, whether of tree or building, lends excitement to a scene; it acts as an exclamation mark in shape, and in character can be varied according to the tree chosen. Trees of rounded contour have none of this dramatic feeling and are in fact usually adjusted by painters to suggest some special quality - grace, opacity, decrepitude, old age or decay - according to the general feeling of the picture, or to convey a sense of a gale of wind. Two other forms of tree are frequently used. One is the pollard, which has rightly come to be associated with streams meandering through meadows, and therefore serves to embellish flat ground. It has been clearly delineated for many years, and is usually shown leaning, which is normal. In the hands of Arthur Rackham and Randolph Caldecott old pollards were made to assume horrific stance and leering faces, long after the advent of the Picturesque! Also associated with tranquil water is the weeping tree, of which the foremost, if not the only, type in pictures is the weeping willow. From time immemorial this tree has come to represent sadness; with its long branches trailing at the water's edge it conjures up tears and melancholy. Therefore it is used by artists as an embellishment to gentle scenes but seldom as an adjunct to a ruined temple, mighty cataract or rocky hill. Venerable oaks or rugged pines are often chosen to give extra vigour to such pictures. Both the oak and the pine excel in this capacity and the latter is one of the most easily recognised trees in English paintings.

Earlier I have mentioned the special value of the ash tree to photographers and artists of all kinds. It is open in habit and therefore does not act as a solid light-excluding screen, and the shape of its leaves can be conveyed to paper fairly simply and obviously. Constable was very successful with his "Study of Ash Trees" and John White Abbott clearly depicts the ash in his "Trees and Rocks in Dovedale"; it is moreover an association which occurs frequently in upland, limestone districts. The fact that the ash bursts into leaf late in the spring gives it a few weeks of pre-eminence, when its silhouette of branches allows the eye to take in beauty through and around it. As Tennyson has it, "... the tender ash delays/To clothe herself when all the woods are green."

Not so do the impenetrable branches of the fully fledged Hornbeam, Sycamore, Sweet Chestnut, beech and elm, whose foliage is usually given a copy-book formula which renders identification - if ever it was intended - very chancy. Trees in the main fulfil two functions in pictures. They may act as a comfortable background, giving depth and perhaps darkness; on the other hand many French paintings of the seventeenth century, particularly by Claude, owe much of their appeal to a great leaning foreground tree interposed between the eye and the light of the sun. Thus the tree would be dark while allowing the sun's rays, or the evening glow, to flood the main scene. This bold foreground placing with all its assets of changing light can be captured in our landscape planting if we follow the precepts laid down in Chapter 3. Willows are particularly useful in showing both light and the passage of the wind, on account of the pale undersides of the leaves; I call to mind their use in Francis Nicholson's views of Stourhead, where they indicate water and marshes and also give diversity to nobler forms of tree growth.

Artists as a rule treat trees as a generalised embellishment to a picture, but sometimes individual specimens are shown. We may look with nostalgia at Constable's superb portrait of an "English Elm at Old Hall Park, East Bergholt", and another, detailed painting of its trunk, and there are many examples in his work of Lombardy Poplars. The studies of the Black Poplar in his "Boat Building", in "The Hay-wain" and in "The Mill Stream", pointed out to me by Edgar Milne-Redhead, are authentic of this noble species in East Anglia. His "Scots Pine and Fir Tree at Hampstead" gives us other clear identifications, as does James Stark's "Trees at Knowle". Constable's "Oak Tree in a Hayfield" is noteworthy in that although the oak is by no means a splendid specimen the drawing conveys very definitely its species. In "A Water-mill at Gillingham, Dorset", the Burdock leaves in the foreground are used in the same way as we often see in eighteenth-century engravings, to give scale.

In pictures there is always – perhaps fortunately – the artists' licence and personality to be taken into account, without which few paintings would retain the compelling magic which is theirs. They are not photographs coldly recording the facts. Both artists and poets place artistry first. Perhaps these very few examples from our immense heritage of paintings will indicate that the choice of a tree or trees for any given place is not to be at the whim of the painter or the planter, but is governed instead by the effect required and also by the suitability to the surroundings.

Turning now to poets, we find that all the artists' thoughts are readily translated into verse, but with two added dimensions, those of sound and fragrance. Trees can be drawn to indicate a rushing wind but we need words to convey the sound.

There is also touch, but this need scarcely delay us because we are concerned almost entirely with the impressions that we gain from trees at a distance. But I should like to record how one great tree-lover, Humphrey Gilbert-Carter, sometime Director of the University Botanic Garden at Cambridge, used to stroke or pat the trunks of trees when taking us round the Garden. Soft or hard, rough or smooth, caressing them provided different sensations which he did his best to convey to us. And in a similar vein Gertrude Jekyll maintained that she could detect under what sort of trees she was standing by the sound of the wind passing through the foliage or the patter of raindrops on the leaves.

It is the pines and the poplars which have inspired poets most in creating their word-pictures for sound. The "gloomy pine" by which is usually meant the Scots Pine, has called for the fullest expression. William Drummond of Hawthornden, in the early seventeenth century, embraces both pine and fir:

> The loud wind through the forest wakes . . .
> And in yon gloomy Pines strange music makes
> The bending Firs a mournful cadence keep.

Pines will grow on poor stony soil and thus often inhabit raised ground, catching the full force of the gale, which nineteenth-century Alexander Smith records:

> In winter, when the dismal rain
>   Came down in slanting lines
> And wind, that grand old harper, smote
>   His thunder-harp of pines.

Pines are not always "gloomy" but there is no doubt about the "sable" (or black) yew, which drives poets to some of their darkest thoughts. The tree whose wind-music summons up a wistful, whispering sadness is the poplar and I think poets usually have in mind the Aspen, whose leaves rattle and sigh at the slightest breeze. Though all poplars have the flattened leaf-stalk which makes the blade so vulnerable to the wind, the Aspen has it in the most extreme form. "The quaking Aspen, light and thin/To th'air light passage gives" comes from Patrick Hannay in the seventeenth century, and John Clare thought the sound so mimics fast-approaching showers "that the plough-boy thinks the rain begun". One would expect to find an example in James Thomson's *The Seasons*:

> A perfect calm; that not a breath
> Is heard to quiver through the closing woods,
> Or rustling turn the many twinkling leaves
> Of Aspen tall . . .

Carrying its message in a different way in former times, the Aspen's light straight-grained timber was prized for arrows.

I have been unable to find any references of importance to the scent of poplars and pines, and certainly not to the sweet strawberry odour given off by Douglas Fir and *Cercidiphyllum* which have more recently regaled us in our gardens – the former on hot summer days and the latter on damp mild autumn days when the leaves are freshly fallen. Fragrance is, however, very much part of our enjoyment of trees; they all smell different and Walt

Whitman refers to "the fragrant pines, and the cedars dusk and dim".

The lime – or linden as it was called in pre-Evelyn days – has a special call on our sense of smell. Matthew Arnold in "The Scholar Gipsy" yearns for

> And air-swept lindens yield
> Their scent, and rustle down their perfum'd showers
> Of bloom on the bent grass where I am laid.

Besides its fragrance and beauty the lime enters into another form of art: it has for long been a favourite of the wood-carver, from Luke Lightfoot and Grinling Gibbons to exponents of today. Descending for a moment from trees to shrubs I am reminded of Robert Bridges's lovely line, "All day in the sweet box tree the bee for pleasure hummeth." Box-wood is prized for its hard smoothness, providing the perfect material for wood-cuts and early printing and also boards for painting. But to return to the lime, John Evelyn quotes from the verse of Abraham Cowley:

> The stately Lime, smooth, gentle, straight and fair
> (With which no other Dryad can compare)
> With verdant locks, and fragrant blossoms deckt,
> Does a large, even, odorate shade project.

All the qualities of the lime tree are gathered into those four lines. No less a grace is found in the "Birch, most shy and lady-like of trees" and "most beautiful of forest trees, the Lady of the Woods". Another fragrant tree of majesty, but often maligned and seldom immortalised in verse, is remembered by Wordsworth with "His seat beneath the honeyed Sycamore, where the bees hum".

There is no doubt that the passage of air through trees brings us great benefits, but let us now leave this pleasant thought, and consider the characters of trees, another favourite theme. Poets, like artists, choose their trees to convey certain impressions. They derive lightness from birches and willows, in contrast to the sturdiness of chestnuts and oaks. As early as the seventeenth century Dryden wrote:

> The monarch oak, the patriarch of trees,
> Shoots, rising up, and spreads by slow degrees;
> Three centuries he grows, and three he stays
> Supreme in state, and in three more decays.

It will be noted that in those days the oak was accorded full masculinity! William Mason echoed this with:

> ... Behold yon Oak
> How stern he frowns, and with his broad brown arms
> Chills the pale plain beneath him.

But apart from the notion of grandeur, the oak was constantly in people's minds as the principal timber for building and enthralled our ancestors because it provided the main means of crossing the oceans. Here is William Mason again:

> These sapling oaks, which at Britannia's call,
> May heave their trunks mature into the main,
> And float the bulwarks of her liberty.

We will let our other superb native tree, the beech, be ushered in by John Gay of *The Beggar's Opera*, where it is found growing together with the oak as Repton would have wished:

> Where the tall oak his spreading arms entwines,
> And with the beech a mutual shade combines.

The brilliant green of the beech in spring has always enthralled us, mainly because, unlike the elm and the oak, its leaves emerge from their quickly elongated buds fully grown and in their silky uniformity make a pretty dappling of colour or shadow. This uniformity is preserved until autumn, when their wonderful colour is taken up by A. E. Housman:

> ... beeches strip in storms for winter
> And stain the wind with leaves.

The roots of the beech, risen above ground, make a remarkable pattern with the fallen leaves, but the smooth grey bark of the trunk has a danger, described by Thomas Campbell:

> ... Youthful lovers in my shade
> Their vows of truth and rapture made.
> And on my trunk's surviving frame
> Carved many a long-forgotten name.

Once again the noted character of a tree, the treachery of elms unexpectedly dropping branches in the still of the day, is to the fore in a poet's mind, in Kipling's lines:

Ellum she hateth mankind, and waiteth
    Till every gust be laid
To drop a limb on the head of him
    That anyway trusts her shade.

Planes and Sycamores are interchangeable for most people except botanists, though there is not much resemblance between them apart from their jagged leaves. The peeling bark of the plane seems to confirm that William Cullen Bryant had this tree in mind when he wrote in "Green River":

Clear are the depths where its eddies play,
And dimples deepen and whirl away;
And the Plane-tree's speckled arms o'ershoot
The swifter current that mines its root.

Our best planes are never far from water or a watery subsoil.

No season is all gloom, as Wordsworth knew when he wrote of the positive character of the Rowan:

... The Mountain Ash
No eye can overlook, when, 'mid a grove
Of yet unfaded trees, she lifts her head,
Deck'd with autumnal berries that outshine
Spring's richest blossom.

Spring is celebrated in these lines extolling the Horse Chestnut:

... Glorious array'd:
For in its honour prodigal nature weaves
    A princely vestment, and profusely showers
O'er its green masses of broad palmy leaves
    Ten thousand waxen pyramidal flowers;
And gay and gracefully its head it heaves
    Into the air, and monarch-like it towers,
Dimming all other trees.

One can sense the glory of the day – a gentle breeze, brilliant sunshine, shadow-dappled lawn or meadow; a different picture from that stormy May day that inspired Housman:

The chestnut casts his flambeaux, and the flowers
    Stream from the hawthorn on the wind away,

The doors clap to, the pane is blind with showers.
> Pass me the can, lad; there's an end of May.

And so we return to the willow, that perpetual symbol of sadness. Thomas Chatterton, who died at eighteen, wrote:

Cold he lies in the grave below:
> My love is dead,
> Gone to his death bed
All under the willow tree.

And there is the old song with the recurring refrain:

To the brook and the willow, that heard him complain,
> Ah! willow, willow!
Poor Colin went weeping and told them his pain;
> Ah! willow, willow!

Thomas Hood took a peaceful view:

And bright and silvery the willows sleep
Over the shady verge – no mad winds tease
Their hoary shade; but quietly they weep
Their sprinkling leaves – half fountains and half trees.

In the use of words to describe melancholy has anyone ever equalled John Keats?

Then in a wailful choir the small gnats mourn
> Among the river sallows.

Though in the main I have quoted from eighteenth-century verse, trees have never been far from poets' thoughts. It comes as something of a surprise that the Picturesque was foreshadowed by the Elizabethan Spenser, long before such things – aweful and horrific – were taken to heart by landscapists, poets and artists.

A huge Oak, dry and dead,
Still clad with reliques of its glories old,
> Lifting to Heaven its aged, hoary head;
Whose foot on earth hath got but feeble hold,
> And, half-disbowelled, stands above the ground;

With wreathed roots, and naked arms,
    And trunk all rotten and unsound.

Anyone who reads John Evelyn's *Silva* will discover a forceful evocation
of the oak as the bulwark of our island fortress. And yet Milton, in the
middle of the seventeenth century, was well aware that we could not cross
the oceans by means of the oak alone; ships needed masts and these for some
time had been imported from Norway, the home of tall firs:

> . . . the tallest Pine
> Hewn on Norwegian hills to be the mast
> Of some great ammiral.

This importation of masts of Norwegian Fir was a lengthy tradition.
Chaucer refers to the "sayling pine", as does Spenser; they both run a
catalogue of trees and their uses. Spenser's includes these lines:

> The sailing pine; the cedar proud and tall;
> The vine-prop elm; the poplar never dry;
> The builder oak, sole King of forests all;
> The aspen good for staves; the cypress funeral;
> . . . the fir that weepeth still;
> The willow, worn of forlorn paramours;
> The yew, obedient to the bencher's will;
> The birch for shafts; the sallow for the mill;
> The myrrh sweet-bleeding in the bitter wound;
> The war-like beech; the ash for nothing ill;
> The fruitful olive; and the plantane round;
> The carver holm; the maple seldom inward sound.

It is a far cry, and a considerable step, from this sort of herbalists' eulogy of
the late sixteenth century to Richard Payne Knight, extoller of the Picturesque two hundred years or so later. Getting thoroughly into his stride in
"The Landscape" he sought to focus the trend of landscape gardening his
way and ignored Humphry Repton:

> Let, then, of oak your general masses rise,
> Where'er the soil its nutriment supplies:
> But if dry chalk and flints, or thirsty sand,
> Compose the substance of your barren land,
> Let the light beech its gay luxuriance shew,
> And o'er the hills its brilliant verdure strew:

No tree more elegant its branches spreads;
None o'er the turf a clearer shadow sheds;
No foliage shines with more reflected lights;
No stem more varied forms and tints unites:
Now smooth, in even bark, aloft it shoots:
Now bulging swells, fantastic as its roots;
While flickering greens, with lightly scattered grey,
Blend their soft colours, and around it play.
But though simplicity the mass pervade,
In groups be gay variety displayed:
Let the rich lime-trees shade the broken mound,
And the thin birch and hornbeam play around;
Willows and alders overhang the stream,
And quiver in the sun's reflected beam.
Let the broad wych your ample lawns divide,
And whittey glitter up the mountain side;
The hardy whittey, that o'er Cambrian snows
Beams its red glare, and in bleak winter glows:
Let the light ash its wanton foliage spread
Against the solemn oak's majestic head;
And where the giant his high branches heaves,
Loose chestnuts interweave their pointed leaves;
While tufted thorns and hazels shoot below,
And yews and hollies deep in shadow grow.

In these few lines a wealth of appreciation and experience is conveyed in assessing the landscape value of the different trees. There is, surely, enough varied beauty in our natives to provide landscape pictures of infinite diversity.

For all his poetry, Knight was, like Repton, a man who understood something also about cultivation and the practical side of things. He prefaced the above lines with some good counsel:

Ere yet the planter undertakes his toil,
Let him examine well his clime and soil;
Patient explore what best with both will suit,
And, rich in leaves, luxuriantly shoot.
For trees, unless in vigorous health they rise,
Can ne'er be grateful objects to the eyes ...

This is not meant to be a comprehensive anthology of poetry about trees. For this you must turn to *The Book of the Tree* by Georgina Mase, where there is a large enough selection to satisfy all. But by the inclusion of these few fragments I have endeavoured to show how trees appeal to all our senses. They are part of our life on earth and we are dependent upon them for the freshness of the air, to say nothing of the uses to us of their wood. Therefore I shall conclude by saying: let us plant more trees, but consider first how their placing will affect our lives and grace this earth. J. H. B. Peel reminded me of Beethoven's remark: "When everything else has failed, there is always the countryside."

BIBLIOGRAPHY

BEAN, W. J., *Trees and Shrubs Hardy in the British Isles.* John Murray, London, Eighth Edition, 1970.

COLVIN, BRENDA, *Land and Landscape.* John Murray, London, 1948.

CROWE, DAME SYLVIA, *The Landscape of Forests and Woods.* Forestry Commission Booklet 44. Her Majesty's Stationery Office, London, 1978.

EDLIN, H. L., *Trees, Woods and Man.* The New Naturalist, Collins, London, 1956.

HADFIELD, MILES, *British Trees.* J. M. Dent, London, 1957.

HADFIELD, MILES, *Landscape with Trees.* Country Life, London, 1967.

HOSKINS, W. G., *The Making of the English Landscape.* Penguin Books, Harmondsworth, 1973.

JOHNS, REV. C. A., *The Forest Trees of Britain.* Society for Promoting Christian Knowledge, London, 1894.

LOUDON, J. C., *An Encyclopaedia of Gardening.* Longman, Rees, Orme, Brown & Green, London, 1827.

MASE, GEORGINA, ed., *The Book of the Tree.* Peter Davies, London, 1927.

MAXWELL, RT. HON. SIR HERBERT, Bt, *Trees, a Woodland Notebook.* James Maclehose, Glasgow, 1915.

MITCHELL, ALAN, *A Guide to the Trees of Britain and Northern Europe.* Collins, London, 1979.

RACKHAM, OLIVER, *Trees and Woodland in the British Landscape.* J. M. Dent, London, 1976.

REPTON, HUMPHRY, *The Art of Landscape Gardening,* ed. John Nolen. Constable, London, 1807.

REPTON, HUMPHRY, *Observations on the Theory and Practice of Landscape Gardening.* J. Taylor, London, 1805.

REPTON, HUMPHRY, *Sketches and Hints on the Theory and Practice of Landscape Gardening.* W. Bulmer, London, 1794.

REPTON, HUMPHRY, and REPTON, J. ADEY, *Fragments on the Theory and Practice of Landscape Gardening.* J. Taylor, London, 1816.

ROBINSON, WILLIAM, *The Garden Beautiful, Home Woods and Home Landscape.* John Murray, London, 1907.

STROUD, DOROTHY, *Humphry Repton.* Country Life, London, 1962.

THOMAS, GRAHAM STUART, *Gardens of the National Trust.* The National Trust, Weidenfeld & Nicolson, London, 1979.

WALSHE, PAUL, and WESTLAKE, CHRISTOPHER, *Tree Guards (Management and Design Notes No. 6), Supplement to Countryside Recreation Review No. 2,* Countryside Commission, London, 1977. Crown Copyright.

INDEX

Page numbers in italics refer to black and white illustrations and captions

TAL-Y-CAFN '47
4